Contents

Introduction

Best wishes to you and your fiancé on your engagement. Now it's time for the exciting task of planning your wedding. Make no mistake, there'll be a lot to remember and a lot to do, but don't be daunted; *The Everything®️ Wedding Checklist* can be a great help.

When should you start looking for your wedding gown? What time was that appointment with the baker? Who was that promising DJ your friends told you about? With this book you won't need to rack your brain for the answers to these and many more questions. Within these pages you'll not only find the answers you need, but a convenient place to keep track of names, appointments, and any other information you'll need to know while planning your wedding.

Whether it's picking a reception site, finding a photographer, choosing flowers, or any of the other million things you'll need to do, this book can tell you when, where, and how to do them. The year-long planning calendar will put you on the right track and the subsequent checklists for each section will help you stay there. In addition, each chapter contains insights and advice on every aspect of your wedding, from finding a gown to picking a limousine.

In short, if you need to be informed about it or reminded to do it in order to plan your ultimate wedding, *The Everything®️ Wedding Checklist* won't let you down.

Remember, you really must adhere to this schedule if you want your wedding to go off without a hitch. Though your tendency may be to procrastinate in the early months, don't! Don't worry, you won't be bored later; there will be plenty to keep your thumbs from twiddling as the wedding date begins to loom large on the horizon. And wouldn't you rather be free to deal with new issues instead of being bogged by tasks that could have been done months ago? Sticking to your schedule is the best and only way to make things go smoothly. And don't forget that starting early will give you the breathing room to take your time and make unrushed choices.

CHAPTER ONE

Off to a
Great Start!

So, you're engaged. Now what? After the dust settles from the whirlwind of excitement and celebrating with family and friends, there are some things you'll have to do to actually get married. Depending upon the type and size wedding you decide to have, you may have lots to do, or tons to do. In any event, the following schedule should give you a general idea of what has to be done, and when you should do it.

Marry me Jennifer!

Six to 12 months before the wedding:

- ☑ Announce engagement
- ☑ Decide on kind of wedding
- ☐ Decide time of day
- ☐ Decide location
- ☑ Set a date
- ☐ Set a budget
- ☐ Select bridal party
- ☑ Plan color scheme
- ☑ Select and order bridal gown
- ☑ Select and order headpiece
- ☑ Select and order shoes
- ☑ Select and order attendants' gowns
- ☑ Start honeymoon planning
- ☑ Go to bridal gift registry
- ☑ Start compiling the guest list
- ☑ Select caterer
- ☑ Select musicians
- ☐ Select florist
- ☑ Select photographer
- ☐ Start planning reception
- ☑ Reserve hall, hotel, etc., for reception

- ☑ Plan to attend premarital counseling at your church, if applicable
- ☑ Select and order wedding rings

Three months before the wedding:
- ☑ Complete guest list
- ☑ Make doctor's appointments *(DENTIST | Herbalist)*
- ☑ Plan to have mothers select attire *LIGHT CANDLES*
- ☑ Select and order invitations
- ☐ Order personal stationery
- ☐ Start compiling trousseau
- ☑ Finalize reception arrangements (rent items now)
- ☑ Make reservations for honeymoon
- ☐ Confirm dress delivery
- ☐ Confirm time and date with florist
- ☐ Confirm time and date with caterer
- ☐ Confirm time and date with photographer
- ☐ Confirm time and date with musicians
- ☐ Confirm time and date with church
- ☐ Discuss transportation to ceremony and reception
- ☑ Order cake
- ☑ Select and order attire for groomsmen
- ☐ Schedule bridesmaids' dress and shoe fittings
  Sharon's Dress | Scarves

Two months before the wedding:
- ☑ Mail all invitations to allow time for R.S.V.P.s
- ☑ Arrange for appointment to get marriage license
- ☐ Finalize honeymoon arrangements *to Hotel PICK UP AIRPORT*

One month before the wedding:
- ☐ Schedule bridal portrait *(us WoeWour Girls)*
- ☑ Reserve accommodations for guests
- ☐ Begin to record gifts received and send thank-you notes
- ☑ Plan rehearsal and rehearsal dinner *NOTE*
- ☐ Purchase gifts for bridal party

- ☐ Purchase gift for fiancé if gifts are being exchanged
- ☐ Schedule final fittings, including accessories and shoes
- ☐ Schedule appointments at beauty salon for attendants
- ☐ Schedule bridesmaids' luncheon or party
- ☐ Arrange for placement of guest book
- ☐ Obtain wedding props, e.g., pillow for ring bearer, candles, etc.
- ☐ Get marriage license

Two weeks before the wedding:

- ☐ Mail bridal portrait with announcement to newspaper
- ☐ Finalize wedding day transportation
- ☐ Arrange to change name on license, social security card, etc.
- ☐ Confirm accommodations for guests
- ☐ Prepare wedding announcements to be mailed after the wedding

One week before the wedding:

- ☐ Start packing for honeymoon
- ☐ Finalize number of guests with caterer
- ☐ Double-check all details with those providing professional services (photographer, videographer, florist, etc.)
- ☐ Plan seating arrangements
- ☐ Confirm desired pictures with photographer
- ☐ Style your hair with headpiece
- ☐ Practice applying cosmetics in proper light
- ☐ Arrange for one last fitting of all wedding attire
- ☐ Make sure rings are picked up and fit properly
- ☐ Confirm receipt of marriage license
- ☐ Rehearsal/rehearsal dinner (one or two days before wedding)

- [ ] Arrange to have the photographer and attendants arrive two hours before ceremony if there are to be prewedding pictures
- [ ] Arrange for music to start one half hour prior to ceremony
- [ ] Arrange to have the mother of the groom seated five minutes before ceremony
- [ ] Arrange to have the mother of the bride seated immediately before the processional
- [ ] Arrange for the aisle runner to be rolled out by the ushers immediately before the processional
- [ ] Arrange and attend the bridesmaids' luncheon

Some General Thoughts

Over the course of your planning, there are a few policies you should adopt to ensure that everything will go smoothly.

🔊 Don't put off until tomorrow what you can do today. A cliché, yes, but nevertheless applicable when it comes to planning a wedding. There will be plenty to do as your wedding grows near; don't make things worse for yourself by leaving everything to the last minute.

🔊 Stick to your budget. If you have a well-thought-out budget, you'll make things a great deal easier on yourself. You won't go into the poorhouse over your wedding, and you won't waste time pursuing options that you can't afford.

🔊 Get everything in writing. There are a lot of crooked people and establishments in the wedding industry just waiting to take advantage of a starry-eyed couple. Don't let them ruin your wedding! Get every aspect of every purchase agreement in writing, so that if things don't come out to your satisfaction, you will have the proper recourse. Another way to keep from being a victim: get references from every single place you're even considering doing business with.

Your Wedding Date

When people learn of your engagement, the first thing you're likely to hear after "Congratulations!" is "So, when's the date?" Until you set a date, you will have no good answer to this question. Worse still, you won't be able to forge ahead with your other planning. Knowing the date is absolutely crucial; it is the linchpin to your entire wedding. When will you need the ceremony and reception sites? How long do you have to find a dress? When will you require the services of paid professionals, such as caterers, photographers, and musicians? These and many other questions will remain unanswered until you've set a date.

To pick a date you can stick to, you'll have to do some serious soul searching. Ask yourself:

🖉 What season do you prefer? Do you want a country garden wedding in the spring? A seaport wedding in the summer? A celebration at a refurbished farmhouse in the fall? Does the season matter to you at all?

🖉 Is there a time of year that your family or the groom's family finds particularly meaningful?

🖉 How much time do you need to plan the wedding?

🖎 Does the availability of a ceremony and reception site coincide with your desired date?

🖎 Are there conflicts that exist for you, your family, or attendants (such as another wedding, a vacation, a graduation, a pregnancy/birth, military commitments)? It's doubtful your matron of honor would enjoy standing beside you in her eighth month wearing a dress that could double for a tent. By the same token, your parents are unlikely to appreciate having to choose between your wedding and your brother's high school graduation.

🖎 How many other couples will be getting married around the same time?

During peak wedding months, there may be a lot of competition for everything from flowers to frosting. Here's the breakdown of what percentage of marriages take place each month:

January – 5 percent
February – 6 percent
March – 6 percent
April – 7 percent
May – 9 percent
June – 11 percent
July – 10 percent
August – 11 percent
September – 10 percent
October – 9 percent
November – 8 percent
December – 8 percent

Your Engagement Ring

If you and your fiancé have set your sights on a diamond engagement ring (or, for that matter, if you plan to purchase a diamond wedding band) and plan to shop for it as a team, make sure you know the four Cs before forking over any of your hard-earned savings. The four Cs are the four marks of a diamond's quality, and the stone you purchase should pass the test in all these categories:

ℬ Clarity: The clarity of a diamond is measured by the number of its flaws or imperfections (either interior or exterior). Clarity, broadly speaking, is the most important factor in determining the beauty of a given stone: a stone with low clarity, for example, will have a number of imperfections when viewed under a gemologist's magnifying glass.

ℬ Cut: The cut of a diamond is the stone's physical configuration, the result of the process whereby the rough gem is shaped. The diamonds you will be shown by a jeweler have had many cuts made on the surface of the stone to shape them and emphasize their brilliance. Common shapes include the "round" (or "brilliant"), pearl shaped, oval, and marquise cuts.

ℬ Color: The color of the diamond is also a major factor in determining its value. Stones that are colorless are considered to be perfect. The object, then, is to find a stone that is as close to colorless as possible—unless, of course, your personal preference dictates otherwise. (Many people prefer to wear stones with a slight discoloration, even though these stones are not—financially, at any rate—worth as much as their higher-quality, colorless counterparts.)

ℬ Carat: The diamond's carat weight refers to the actual size of the stone. (Unlike the carat weight of gold, the carat weight of a diamond is simply a physical measure of the weight of the item in question—and not a measure of quality or purity.) Bear in mind that carat weight alone is not necessarily an indicator of price or value. A three-quarter-carat-weight, colorless, flawless diamond will almost certainly be appraised higher than a two-carat-weight stone with several flaws and a murky, yellowish tint.

Jewelry Shopping Tips

Your first step in the search for a ring should be to consult with a reputable jeweler. Referrals from experienced family and friends are probably the best way to find someone trustworthy. Should your social circle not yield many results, go ahead and pick a store that appeals to you, stocks jewelry in your price range, and is a member of the American Gem Society. But while members of the AGS must meet high standards of quality and reputability, you should still avoid taking any chances by . . .

ℬ Shopping around. Even if you fall head over heels in love with the first ring you set eyes on, a little perspective never hurt anyone. Comparing selections from other jewelers should give you a better idea of fair pricing as well as your options. Beware of shops that pressure you to buy on the spot.

ℬ Negotiating. Don't hesitate to ask if the price is negotiable. Like car salespeople, jewelry salespeople expect to do their fair share of haggling.

ℬ Making the final sale contingent upon your taking the ring to an appraiser of your choice to verify value and price. Don't worry, there's nothing rude about assuming this course of action, as there are quite a few unscrupulous jewelers who will try to dupe you into buying a ring for much more than it's worth by having their appraiser (or one they recommend) "confirm" the ring's inflated value.

🪔 Getting a purchase agreement that includes stipulations for sizing and potential return. Does the store offer a money-back guarantee if the ring is returned within the designated time frame? Also, any sizing, tightening, or cleaning required during the first six months of ownership should be free.

🪔 Getting a written appraisal and insurance. It's not romantic, but insurance purposes demand that you get a written appraisal that describes the ring and cites its value. Insure your ring under your homeowner's or renter's policy.

Choosing Your Engagment Ring

Jewelry store #1:_____

Address:_____

Telephone number: _____

Sales representative:_____

Store hours:_____

Notes: _____

_____

_____

Your Wedding Party

As soon as you and your fiancé figure out who you want in your wedding party, get on out there and ask them. Giving people advance notice allows them the time to prepare for the extensive financial and time commitments involved in a wedding. It also gives you the breathing room to find replacements if your first choices can't accept.

When deciding who to cast in the role of wedding party attendants, it's wise to consider the responsibilities that go along with each job. Feel free to make copies of these lists and hand them out to your would-be attendants to clear up any confusion they may have about their duties.

Engagement Ring Table

STONE:	#1	#2	#3
Jewelry store			
Clarity			
Cut			
Color			
Carats			
Other stones (if applicable)			
Setting			
Notes			
Price per carat			
Tax, other charges			
TOTAL PRICE			

Final choice (stone number from above): _____

Ring size: _____

Order date: _____ Date Ready: _____

Deposit amount: _____ Due date: _____

Balance: _____ Due date: _____

Notes: _____

_____

_____

The maid/matron of honor:

- Helps the bride with addressing envelopes, recording wedding gifts, shopping, and other pre-wedding tasks
- Arranges a bridal shower
- Helps the bride arrange her train and veil at the altar
- Brings the groom's ring to the ceremony site
- Holds the bride's bouquet while she exchanges rings with the groom
- Signs the wedding certificate
- Stands in the receiving line (optional)
- Holds the groom's wedding ring
- Makes sure the bride looks perfect for all the pictures
- Dances with the best man during the attendants' dance at the reception
- Participates in the bouquet toss, if single

The bridesmaids:

- Help organize and run the bridal shower
- Assist the bride and maid of honor with prewedding errands or tasks
- Stand in the receiving line (optional)
- Help the bride get dressed and ready on the wedding day
- Participate in the bouquet toss, if single

The best man:

- Organizes the bachelor party
- Drives the groom to the ceremony
- Brings the bride's ring to the ceremony site
- Gives the officiant his fee immediately before or after the ceremony (provided by the groom's family)

- Gives other service providers such as the chauffeur their fees (optional)
- Returns the groom's attire (if rented)
- Oversees the transfer of gifts to a secure location after reception
- Helps the groom get ready and arrive on time for every wedding-related function
- Holds the bride's ring during the ceremony
- Signs the marriage license as a witness
- Escorts the maid of honor in the recessional
- Sits for pictures with the wedding party and the groom
- Dances with the maid of honor during the attendants' dance at the reception
- Usually sits to the right of the bride at the head table
- Gives the first toast at the reception
- May drive the couple to the reception and/or the hotel if there is no hired driver
- Helps out when the groom is in need of moral support or words of wisdom, or assistance of any kind.

The ushers:

- Arrive at the wedding location early to help with setup
- Attend to last-minute tasks such as lighting candles, tying bows on reserved rows of seating, etc.

🪢 Escort guests to their seats as follows:
  • Ask if they are guests of the bride or groom. If
    they are with the bride, they should be seated
    at the left side of the church (facing the altar).
    If with the groom, then they should be seated
    to the right. The reverse is true for Reform and
    Conservative Jewish weddings.
  • Seat the eldest guests first if a large group arrives.
  • Escort female guests with right arm as her
    escort follows, or lead a couple to their seat
  • Distribute programs to guests after they have
    been seated.
  • Balance out the guests by asking arriving guests
    if they wouldn't mind sitting on the other (less
    filled) side.
  • After the guests have been seated, escort spe-
    cial guests to their seats in this order (unless
    otherwise directed by the bridal couple):
      1. general special guests
      2. grandmothers of the bride and groom
      3. groom's mother
      4. bride's mother
🪢 Roll out aisle runner immediately before processional
🪢 Help decorate newlyweds' car (optional)
🪢 Collect discarded programs and articles from the
   pews after the ceremony
🪢 Direct guests to the reception and hand out
   preprinted maps and directions to those who
   need them
🪢 Assist in gathering the wedding party for photographs

The Mother of the Bride:

Though you may not realize it, the mother of the bride
is considered to be part of the wedding party. After all, your

father gets his moment in the sun when he walks you down the aisle—why not the woman who gave you life? At the beginning of the ceremony, the mother is the last person seated before the processional begins. But, like your attendants, she has plenty to do before the wedding, including:

- Helping the bride in choosing her gown and accessories, and in assembling a trousseau
- Helping the bride select bridesmaids' attire
- Coordinating her own attire with the mother of the groom
- Working with the bride and the groom's family to assemble a guest list and seating plan
- Helping address and mail invitations
- Helping the attendants coordinate the bridal shower
- Assisting the bride in any of the hundreds of things she may need help with before the ceremony
- Occupying a place of honor at the ceremony
- Standing at the beginning of the receiving line
- In most instances, acting as hostess of the reception
- Occupying a seat of honor at the parents' table

Maid/matron of honor: _____

Phone: _____

Address: _____

_____

Bridesmaid: _____

Phone: _____

Address: _____

_____

Bridesmaid: _____

Phone: _____

Address: _____

_____

Bridesmaid:_____

Phone: _____

Address: _____

_____

Bridesmaid:_____

Phone: _____

Address: _____

_____

Best man:_____

Phone: _____

Address: _____

_____

Usher: _____

Phone: _____

Address: _____

_____

Usher: _____

Phone: _____

Address: _____

_____

Usher: _____

Phone: _____

Address: _____

_____

Usher: _____

Phone: _____

Address: _____

_____

Flower girl: _____
Phone: _____
Address: _____
_____

Ring bearer: _____
Phone: _____
Address: _____
_____

Additional special attendants: _____
_____
_____
_____

Gifts for Party Members

Bestowing gifts upon your wedding attendants is the most popular way to say thank-you for all the work, time, and money that these kind souls have put into your wedding. While it's common to give all the bridesmaids and groomsmen the same gift to avoid any resentment or hurt feelings, you can always individualize a little. These tokens of appreciation are disbursed during the rehearsal dinner, so you have some time to shop around for just the right items. The following are some of the more popular gift ideas:

For the bridesmaids:

- Jewelry (possibly something they can wear for the wedding such as earrings or a bracelet)
- Datebook
- Stationery
- Perfume
- Beauty product gift pack
- Jewelry box

- Monogrammed purse mirrors
- Gift certificate (to a bed and bath shop, for instance)

For the groomsmen:
- Monogrammed money clip or key chain
- Datebook
- Pen set
- Cologne
- Silk tie
- Travel or shaving kit
- Gift certificate (to a sporting goods store, for instance)
- Something related to a favorite hobby of the groomsman

The Budget

A budget is the nasty little detail that has a very big influence on your wedding. Your budget (if you stick to it) will dictate the size and style of your wedding, as well as all the other little extras such as flowers, music, photography, video, transportation, and so on.

The first step toward figuring your budget is to sit down with everyone who may be contributing monetarily—your groom, your parents, his parents—and discuss the kind of wedding you'd like to have. Traditionally, the bride's family bears the brunt of the wedding expenses and the groom's picks up the tab for a few select things, but that is by no means set in stone anymore. These days it is not uncommon for the bride and groom to be responsible for the majority of the wedding expenses.

The traditional expenses of the bride's family:

- Bride's wedding gown and accessories
- Fee for ceremony location
- All reception costs (location rental, food, decorations, etc.)
- Flowers for ceremony and reception
- Music
- Photography (and video)
- Transportation (limousine rental, etc.)
- The groom's wedding ring
- Housing for bridesmaids
- Gifts for bridesmaids
- Invitations, reception cards, and announcements
- The groom's gift

The traditional expenses of the groom's family:

- The bride's wedding and engagement ring
- Marriage license
- Officiant's fee
- Housing for ushers
- Gifts for ushers
- Part of the bachelor party (with part of the expense being borne by the groom's friends)
- The bride's gift
- The bride's bouquet
- The bride's going-away corsage (optional)
- Mothers' and grand- mothers' corsages
- Boutonnieres for groom's wedding party
- The rehearsal dinner
- The honeymoon

The traditional expenses of the maid/matron of honor and bridesmaids:

- Their dresses and accessories
- A gift for the couple
- A shower gift
- A contribution to the bridal shower
- Transportation to and from the wedding

The traditional expenses of the best man and ushers/groomsmen:

- Their clothing rental (tuxedo, suit)
- A gift for the couple
- A contribution to the cost of the bachelor party
- Transportation to and from the wedding

If you have the funds available to finance the wedding of your dreams, consider yourself very lucky. But if you find yourself a few dollars short of your dream, don't despair! There are compromises and cuts you can make that will have little or no effect on you or your guests' enjoyment of the day. Have your invitations offset-printed instead of engraved; hold a buffet instead of a sit-down dinner; limit the use of elaborate flowers.

Ultimately, you'll need to prioritize the areas of your wedding so that you can spend money on what's most important to you, on the things you will carry with you from the wedding into your future. Be willing to drop the notion of serving steak at the reception in order to afford a good photographer. What makes your wedding memorable is the love and the people, not the elaborate extras.

Tipping Guidelines

Even the most budget-conscious brides and grooms often overlook one very substantial expense—tips! Depending on the size of your reception and your reception location, tipping can easily add from a few hundred to a few thousand dollars to your costs. Many wedding professionals even include a gratuity in their contract, and then expect an additional tip at the reception. As a result, whom to tip and how much to tip can often be perplexing dilemmas. Although tipping is, for the most part, expected, it is never required—it is simply an extra reward for extraordinary service. Exactly how much or whom you tip is completely at your discretion. The following are simply guidelines, not rules:

    ❧ Caterers and reception site managers usually have gratuities of 15–20 percent included in their contracts. These are usually paid in advance by the host of the reception. If the caterer or manager has been exceptionally helpful, you may wish to give him or her an additional tip, usually $1–$2 per guest.

    ❧ Wait staff usually receive 15–20 percent of the food bill. Caterers sometimes include this gratuity in their contract. But if the tip is not included, give the tip to the head waiter or maitre d' during the reception.

    ❧ Bartenders should be tipped 15–20 percent of the total bar bill. If their gratuity is already included in the catering contract, an additional tip of 10 percent is common. It should be paid by the host during the reception. Don't allow the bartender to accept tips from guests; ask him to put up a small sign that says, "No tipping, please."

    ❧ Restroom, coat check, or parking attendants should be prepaid by the host, usually $1–$2 per guest or car. Ask the staff not to accept tips from guests.

Limousine drivers usually receive 15–20 percent of the bill. Any additional tips are at the host's discretion.

 Musicians or DJs may be tipped if their performance was exceptional. Tips usually run about $25 per band member. DJs are tipped about 15–20 percent of their fee.

 Florists, photographers, and bakers are not usually tipped; you simply pay a flat fee for their services.

 An officiant is never tipped; he or she receives a flat fee for performing the service. A religious officiant may ask for a small donation, around $20, for his or her house of worship, but a civil officiant is not allowed to accept tips.

Wedding Budget Worksheet

Item	Projected Cost*	Deposit Paid	Balance Due	Who Pays
WEDDING CONSULTANT				
Fee ✳	✓			
Tip (usually 15–20%)	✓			
PREWEDDING PARTIES				
Engagement				
(if hosted by bride & groom)				
Site rental	✓			
Equipment rental	✓			
Invitations	✓			
Food ✳	✓			
Beverages ✳	✓			
Decorations	✓			
Flowers	✓			
Party favors	✓			
Bridesmaids' party/luncheon ✳	✓			
Rehearsal dinner				
(if hosted by bride & groom)				
Site rental	✓			
Equipment rental	✓			
Invitations INFO LETTER	15 00			
Food	500 00			
Decorations	⬭			
Flowers	✓			
Party favors	✓			
Weekend wedding parties				

MARSHA

KRISHA

60·

* including tax, if applicable

Item	Projected Cost	Deposit Paid	Balance Due	Who Pays
CEREMONY				
Location fee	300			
Officiant's fee	✓			
Donation to church (optional, amnt varies)	✓			
Organist				
Tip (amount varies)				
Other musicians	200			
Tip (amount varies)				
Program				
Aisle runner	20			
BUSINESS AND LEGAL MATTERS				
Marriage license	30			
Blood test (if applicable)	⬭			
WEDDING JEWELRY				
Engagement ring	2600			
Bride's wedding band	500			
Groom's wedding band	500			
BRIDE'S FORMAL WEAR				
Wedding gown				
Alterations				
Undergarments (slip, bustier, hosiery, etc.)				
Headpiece				
Shoes				
Jewelry (excluding engagement and wedding rings)				

APRIL

JILL - $

Item	Projected Cost	Deposit Paid	Balance Due	Who Pays
Purse (optional)				
Cosmetics, or makeup stylist				
Hair stylist				
Going-away outfit	✓			
Going-away accessories	✓			
Honeymoon clothes	✓			

GROOM'S FORMAL WEAR

Item	Projected Cost	Deposit Paid	Balance Due	Who Pays
Tuxedo	100			
Shoes	✓			
Going-away outfit	✓			
Honeymoon clothes	✓			

GIFTS

Item	Projected Cost	Deposit Paid	Balance Due	Who Pays
Bride's Attendants	175			
Groom's Attendants	175			
Bride (optional)				
Groom (optional)				
other	160			

RECEPTION

Item	Projected Cost	Deposit Paid	Balance Due	Who Pays
Site rental				
Equipment rental (chairs, tent, etc.)				
Decorations				
Servers, bartenders				
Wine service for cocktail hour				
Hors d'oeuvres				
Entrees				

GIFTS →

WEDDING PLANNER
GUEST BOOK
PROGRAMS - 2
USHERS - 2

RING BEARER
FLOWER GIRL
GIFT TABLE - 2
PARENTS - 4

Item	Projected Cost	Deposit Paid	Balance Due	Who Pays
Meals for hired help				
Nonalcoholic beverages				
Wine				
Champagne				
Liquor				
Dessert				
Toasting glasses				
Guest book and pen				
Place cards	~~25~~			
Printed napkins	✓			
Party favors (matches, chocolates, etc.)				
Box or pouch for envelope gifts				
Tip for caterer or banquet manager (usually 15–20%)				
Tip for servers, bartenders (usually 15–20% total)				
PHOTOGRAPHY AND VIDEOGRAPHY				
Engagement portrait				
Wedding portrait				
Wedding proofs				
Photographer's fee				
Wedding prints				
Album				
Mother's albums				
Extra prints				
Videographer's fee				
Videotape				

(handwritten margin notes, left side:) ASK RECEPTION, FRAN, TERESA S., KRISTA S.

(handwritten note next to "Party favors":) FLOWERS

Item	Projected Cost	Deposit Paid	Balance Due	Who Pays
RECEPTION MUSIC				
Musicians for cocktail hour	✓			
Tip (optional, up to 15%)	✓			
Live Band	✓			
Tip (optional, usually $25 per band member)	✓			
Disc Jockey	(circled)			
Tip (optional, usually 15–20%)				
FLOWERS AND DECORATIONS				
Flowers for wedding site				
Decorations for wedding site				
Bride's bouquet				
Bridesmaids' flowers				
Boutonnieres				
Corsages				
Flowers for reception site				
Potted plants				
Table centerpieces				
Head table				
Cake table				
Decorations for reception				
WEDDING INVITATIONS AND STATIONERY				
Invitations				
Announcements				
Thank-you notes				
Calligrapher				
Postage				

(Handwritten marginal notes: "KRISTA, JILL.", "TERESA K", "ARCHIVERS", "KRISTA S")

Item	Projected Cost	Deposit Paid	Balance Due	Who Pays
WEDDING CAKE				
Wedding cake				
Groom's cake				
Cake top and decorations				
Flowers for cake				
Cake serving set				
Cake boxes				
WEDDING TRANSPORTATION				
Limousines or rented cars				
Parking				
Tip for drivers (15–20%)				
GUEST ACCOMMODATIONS				
GUEST TRANSPORTATION				
HONEYMOON				
Transportation				
Accommodations				
Meals				
Spending Money				
ADDITIONAL EXPENSES (LIST BELOW)				
TOTAL OF ALL EXPENSES				

CHAPTER TWO

The Guest List

Compiling a list of names to invite to the wedding can be a smooth, effortlessly enjoyable process—that is, if you have a tension-free family life, an endless supply of wedding funds, unlimited reception space, and a magician who'll whip up a seating plan that pleases everyone. If you're not one of the lucky .0001 percent of the population who fits into this category, hammering out your guest list can be a process challenging enough to merit inclusion on your professional resume. We can just see it now, "Streamlined wedding ceremony guest list" ranked along with all your other accomplishments.

If money is no object, and the size of your reception site dwarfs the Taj Mahal, you should be able to invite as many people as your hospitable heart desires. But, if like most of us you're on a budget, you'll have to do some fancy footwork.

- Split the list three ways: the bride's parents, the groom's parents and the couple each get to invite one-third of the guest list.
- Start out by listing everyone you'd ideally like to have: perhaps the total number is not beyond your reach.
- Set up boundaries if the list is too long

Setting Your Boundaries

If you want to drastically cut down your number of guests, drawing names out of a hat and axing anyone whose name comes up is not the best way to go. Instead, consider subjecting your guest list to a set of well-defined rules and policies. Just remember, you must apply all rules across the board.

Making exceptions for certain people is the single best way to offend others and create more headaches for yourself.

Consider implementing the following policies:

🔗 No children: That you're not inviting children is usually implied to parents by the fact that, hard as they may search, their children's names do not appear anywhere on the invitation. Just to be safe, however, make sure your mother (and anyone else who might be questioned) is aware of your policy. What's the cut-off point between children and young adults? It's up to you to pick an age, but 18 and 16 are common cut-offs.

🔗 No children at the meal: Same as above, except you're only excluding the little urchins from the meal itself and not from the post-dining festivities. Letting the children come by after dinner to enjoy the fun should soften the blow of excluding all children and might even add some extra spark to the reception.

🔗 No coworkers: If you were counting on talking to people at the wedding to help strengthen business ties, this may not be the best option. But if you do need to cut somewhere, and you feel comfortable excluding work acquaintances, this may be the way to go.

🔗 No thirds, fourths, or twice-removeds: If you have a large immediate family and a thousand nearest and dearest friends, you may want to exclude distant relatives from the guest list. Again, be consistent. As long as your third cousins don't have to hear that your second cousins twice removed have been invited, they should understand your need to cut costs.

🔗 Ceremony, but no reception: If you both feel it's important to have a large guest list, you may want to consider inviting more distant relatives and less intimate friends to the ceremony only. To do this, you'll need to order separate reception cards that correspond with the invitations to the ceremony. For the guests who will be invited to the ceremony only, simply omit this card. (Note: While this option may help cut costs, it could also leave the ceremony-only people feeling more slighted than if they hadn't been invited at all. After all, the party is the big attraction—no matter how touching or beautiful your ceremony is.)

No "and guest": While you will certainly want to allow any "attached" guests to bring their significant others, the same kindness does not necessarily need to extend to unattached guests. In other words, if you're on a tight budget and some guests are not part of an established couple, they can go stag and hang with the rest of the swinging singles. If you can't afford to invite single guests with a date, they will almost certainly understand. Remember, however, that married and engaged guests must always be invited along with their spouses and fiancés. Likewise, each of your attendants should be given the option to bring a guest, even if they're not involved in a relationship. They've worked hard and they deserve it.

No return invitations: If a distant relative or acquaintance invited you to his or her wedding, this does not automatically oblige you to return the favor. These people will understand if you make them aware that you're cutting costs and having a small affair. If people approach you and assume they're being invited when they're not, be honest with them—and do so quickly. Don't go home and stew for weeks about how to break the bad news. Waiting only serves to make the situation even more awkward, leading the uninvited to wonder what they may have done to offend you in the interim. The best approach is to be honest right from the get go; tell them you'd love to have them, but you're having a small wedding and it's impossible to invite everyone on your wish list. It may be a little awkward, but it beats dashing expectations down the line.

~ No regrets: Because it's realistic to anticipate some regrets (on average, about 20 to 25 percent of invited guests will be unable to attend), you and your fiancé may decide to send a second mailing of invitations to people on a wish list. If so, your first mailing should be sent 10 to 12 weeks before the wedding date; the second should be sent out no later than five weeks prior.

Making Your List, Checking It Twice

You should check to make sure that all the following information is correct before mailing any invitations. If you're not 100 percent sure on any point, don't hesitate to ask someone who is in the know, or even ask the person in question.

- [ ] Spelling of names
- [ ] Titles (doctors, military personnel, etc.)
- [ ] Addresses
- [ ] Names of significant others
- [ ] Phone numbers (just in case you need to call a late RSVPer, or if any of your friends or family want to contact guests to invite them to showers or other parties in your honor)

Welcoming the Out-of-Towners

Out-of-town shouldn't mean out-of-mind. Since your long distance friends and relatives will be going a long way for your reception, you should try to make things as pleasant and convenient for them as possible. Here are just a few things you can do to make their lives as easy as possible:

🖋 Start by helping the out-of-towners find a place to hang their hats over the course of their stay, whether with family members, friends, or local hotels.

🖋 Make hotel reservations for out-of-town guests, or at the very least, provide these guests with enough information to make their own arrangements. Generally, guests pay for their own lodging (unless either the bride's or groom's family can offer to pick up the tab).

🖋 Check on group rates, to see whether your hotel will offer a lower rate for a group of rooms. Grouping out-of-town guests in one hotel boasts several advantages: the group rates will lighten the burden to their pockets; they can mingle with the other guests during the downtime between wedding events; and they can carpool to and from the festivities.

🖋 Include a note with the invitation. It should list several lodging options, detail the prices and any special features of each place, as well as inform the guests of where it is that you're attempting to coordinate group rates. This way you're assuming nothing about your guest's financial situation—after all, their own particular budget may be more in keeping with Motel 6 than the Four Seasons.

❧ Finances permitting, go the extra mile once you figure out where your guests will be staying and arrange to have a bottle of wine or a fruit basket awaiting their arrival at the hotel room.

❧ Invite the out-of-towners in question to your rehearsal dinner or any other wedding events scheduled to take place while they're in town. This will let them know that the trip was worthwhile and that they've truly been missed.

❧ Don't forget to enclose detailed maps to all the events for those unfamiliar with the area. You don't want guests to have traveled across all that country to make it to your wedding only to miss the event because they got lost a few miles from the ceremony site.

❧ Consider putting a trustworthy friend or relative in charge of herding up the out-of-town group and transporting them from place to place. This person would also be in charge of airport pickups and drop-offs.

❧ For those out-of-town guests who are bringing children along for the ride, but not for the reception, talk about finding a babysitter well in advance. (Some churches have babysitters on hand.) Also, children who are not going to the ceremony/reception can still be invited to the rehearsal dinner.

Wedding Guest Checklist

RSVP	Name	Address
❑	1.	
❑	2.	
❑	3.	
❑	4.	
❑	5.	
❑	6.	
❑	7.	
❑	8.	
❑	9.	
❑	10.	
❑	11.	
❑	12.	
❑	13.	
❑	14.	
❑	15.	
❑	16.	
❑	17.	
❑	18.	
❑	19.	
❑	20.	
❑	21.	
❑	22.	
❑	23.	
❑	24.	
❑	25.	

RSVP	NAME	ADDRESS
❑	26.	
❑	27.	
❑	28.	
❑	29.	
❑	30.	
❑	31.	
❑	32.	
❑	33.	
❑	34.	
❑	35.	
❑	36.	
❑	37.	
❑	38.	
❑	39.	
❑	40.	
❑	41.	
❑	42.	
❑	43.	
❑	44.	
❑	45.	
❑	46.	
❑	47.	
❑	48.	
❑	49.	
❑	50.	

RSVP	NAME	ADDRESS
☐	51.	
☐	52.	
☐	53.	
☐	54.	
☐	55.	
☐	56.	
☐	57.	
☐	58.	
☐	59.	
☐	60.	
☐	61.	
☐	62.	
☐	63.	
☐	64.	
☐	65.	
☐	66.	
☐	67.	
☐	68.	
☐	69.	
☐	70.	
☐	71.	
☐	72.	
☐	73.	
☐	74.	
☐	75.	

RSVP	NAME	ADDRESS
☐	76.	
☐	77.	
☐	78.	
☐	79.	
☐	80.	
☐	81.	
☐	82.	
☐	83.	
☐	84.	
☐	85.	
☐	86.	
☐	87.	
☐	88.	
☐	89.	
☐	90.	
☐	91.	
☐	92.	
☐	93.	
☐	94.	
☐	95.	
☐	96.	
☐	97.	
☐	98.	
☐	99.	
☐	100.	

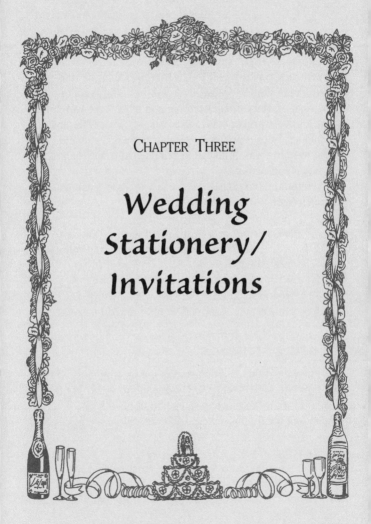

CHAPTER THREE

Wedding Stationery/ Invitations

While you can hire a private printer to create your wedding invitations, the most likely source for your invites is a local stationery or card store. There, you'll find sample catalogs filled with dozens upon dozens of invitation styles, designs, and phrases. These stores are supplied by a few large manufacturers who seem to have the invitation market cornered these days. Because of their size and the volume they deal in, these manufacturers can offer more variety than a private printer—often at a cheaper price. The upside to smaller, private printers: they can do engraving (the most elegant form of invitation printing) and they can work in multiple ink colors.

Here are some basic questions you should ask yourself before ordering your wedding invitations.

- What is the overall style and level of formality of the wedding? (Your invitations should reflect these things.)
- What do you want the invitation to say? How do you want the information worded?
- How do you want the words printed on the paper?

Printing Methods

The answer to this last question is not as simple as whipping out the old Bic ballpoint and going to work. There are a number of more elegant options to choose from, depending upon your budget and your style preferences.

Engraving

As mentioned, engraving is the most elegant way of putting words on paper; unfortunately, it's also the most expensive. The paper is "stamped" from the back by metal plates the printer creates, which raise the letters up off of the paper as they are printed.

Thermography

This is the printing method used by most of the larger invitation printers. About half the price of engraving, thermography uses a method of heated ink printing that creates a look almost indistinguishable from engraving. Not surprisingly, it's quite popular.

Calligraphy

Calligraphy is that very fancy and intricate black script. Technically, calligraphy is done only by calligraphers who are trained in the art form. These people tend to charge a lot of money to perform their art, but don't rule out calligraphy yet. Some printers are now able to reproduce calligraphy by means of a computer program, which is faster—and cheaper—than the human hand. If your stationery store can't point you in the direction of a good calligrapher, check the local Yellow Pages; for computer generated calligraphy, your best bet is a small private printer.

Offset printing

Offset printing, also known as flat printing, is the most common form of printing. Though not as fancy as any of the other options, it is, as mentioned, the only form of printing that allows you to work with multiple ink colors. If you're interested in having your invitations done by the offset method, chances are you'll have to find a small private printer, as the larger ones tend to stick with thermography.

Hand-written invitations

If you are having 50 or fewer guests at your wedding, it is perfectly acceptable to write out your invitations by hand. The only requirement here: whoever is going to do the writing should have legible handwriting.

In addition to these printing methods, there are hundreds of different styles and typefaces to choose from. Take your time and pick a design you really like.

Note: Most invitation packages include response cards and reception cards, but check to make sure that you'll be getting them.

Stationery store (or printer): _____

Address: _____

_____

Phone: _____

Contact person: _____

Number of invitations: _____

Delivery date: _____ Price: _____

Address for Success

Once you've picked out your invitations, sit down with your groom and figure out how many you will need to order. Add 50 or more to your final total before you turn in your order. It's safe to say you (and whoever's helping you) will probably make some mistakes addressing the invitations—and, anyway, you might want to save a few as souvenirs of the big day.

Place your order at least three months before the wedding. If you're really pressed for time, ask to get your envelopes in advance so that you can start addressing them while you're waiting for the invitations to be printed.

Make sure you receive a sample of everything before the full order is printed so that you can proof read it beforehand. Check carefully for typos and spelling errors.

You Will Need

Before you can get started on the invitations, you must have the proper equipment. Here are the tools of the invitation-writers' trade:

- Several black pens
- Several friends and/or family members with good penmanship
- Plenty of food, drink, money, and whatever else it will take to bribe friends and/or family members into helping you
- Stamps
- Invitations and envelopes

Guidelines

There are certain guidelines that you may want to follow when it comes to addressing your invitations.

- Use black ink only.
- Don't typewrite the envelopes or use premade labels. Write everything out by hand.
- Make sure that the same person who's writing on the inside of the invitation addresses the outer envelope.

And about those outer envelopes . . .

- Always address people formally as Mrs., Mr., Ms., unless you feel comfortable enough with them to use names only.
- With the exception of Mr., Mrs., and the like, do not use abbreviations.
- If you opt for a formal means of address, refer to a married couple as "Mr. and Mrs. Stephen Michael McGill."
- If you prefer a more casual means of address, you might refer to a married couple as "Linda and Stephen McGill."

Whether you go with formal or casual is up to you. Only you know your friends and family well enough to say which way is best.

For some couples, you may have to use something like this: "Ms. Linda Ann Smith and Mr. Stephen McGill"

If you are inviting the whole family, simply include the phrase "and family" after the parents' names.

And the inner envelopes?

General address can be more casual: "Mr. and Mrs. McGill" or "Linda and Stephen."

For the whole family: "Mr. and Mrs. McGill, Andrea, Paul, and Meg" or "Linda, Stephen, Andrea, Paul, and Meg."

Anyone over the age of 18 should receive a separate invitation.

Even though the groom's parents already know the specifics of the wedding, send them an invitation anyway.

Pack 'Em up and Ship 'Em Out

Chances are you'll sit down with your invitations, your response cards, your reception cards, and your return envelopes and wonder how the heck you're going to fit all that in one envelope without unsightly lumps. Well, here's how.

1. Place the response card faceup under the flap of the response card envelope.
2. Place a small piece of tissue paper over the lettering on the invitation.
3. Put any extra enclosures (reception cards, maps, directions) inside the invitation.
4. Put the response card and envelope inside the invitations as well. The lettering should be facing upward.
5. Place the invitation inside of the inner envelope with the lettering facing the back flap. Don't seal this envelope.
6. Put the inner envelope inside the outer envelope; again, the writing on the inner envelope should face the flap of the outer envelope.
7. Seal the outer envelope. Make sure the envelope is properly addressed and contains your return address.
8. Stamp and mail.
9. Note: Because of heavy paper and inserts your invitations may require more than standard first-class stamps. A standard first-class stamp will suffice for the return envelope—but remember, you have to provide this stamp as well.

Additional Stationery

Your business with the stationery store (or private printer) usually doesn't end with the invitations. You'll probably be needing thank-you notes, which most couples choose to have done professionally—although it's also appropriate to send notes on personal stationery.

Below is a list of other stationery items you might need to order, depending on your situation—and your budget.

- [ ] Printed directions and/or maps
- [ ] Announcements
- [ ] Ceremony cards (if your ceremony is in a public place)
- [ ] Pew cards (to reserve pews for special family members and friends)
- [ ] Rain cards (to notify guests of an alternate location in the event—oh no!—of rain)
- [ ] Ceremony programs
- [ ] At-home cards (to announce your new address)
- [ ] Name cards (to let the world know if you've taken your new husband's name, kept yours, hyphenated, or whatever)
- [ ] New personal stationery (modified with your name change)
- [ ] Cocktail napkins featuring the names of you and your groom along with your wedding date
- [ ] Matchbooks or boxes
- [ ] Boxes for the groom's cake

CHAPTER FOUR

Bridal Registry

*H*ere's a way to have a say in the gifts you'll get. There's really no need to await each new package with horror, afraid it will contain some tacky atrocity. Why not fill out a gift registry at your favorite store—and await each present with breathless anticipation. The registry is a great thing for your guests, too, they won't have to wrack their brains thinking of an appropriate gift.

When making your wedding gift list . . .

- Shop with your groom so that you make choices together.
- Consider registering at two stores to give wider price range to your guests.
- Discuss return policies with the bridal registrar.
- Ask for a preprinted listing of gifts and household items the store offers.
- List all pattern numbers and color choices.
- Inform your family and friends where you're registered.
- Have the store suggest that everyone send their gifts to your home rather than bring them to the reception.
- Inquire about a temporary insurance policy that will cover the gifts while they're being displayed in your home.
- Ask a reliable friend to transport any gifts from the reception site to your home.
- Remember that, if the wedding is temporarily postponed, all gifts are kept. If the wedding is cancelled, all gifts must be returned. Inform everyone of the cancellation. (But there's no need to give messy details.)

The Trousseau and Beyond

The idea of a registry is to provide the bride with a trousseau, or the things that she and her husband will probably need during their first year. The word trousseau is a throwback to a time when brides brought their own "things" with them into their new home: doilies, fine linens, lingerie, and other such personal items. The small bundle of stuff was called a trousseau. In time, the standard dowry eclipsed what one could carry in a small bundle, but the name stuck just the same.

The days of dowries may have passed (at least in this country), but the need for a new bride to begin her marriage with a "hope chest" has not. Although in olden times the bride and her mother were responsible for filling the hope chest, modernity has spread the duty to include family and friends. The point of the exercise is to help the couple start building a home. The trousseau includes:

- Bed linen (at least three sets for the master bedroom and two for the guest room)
    - Fitted sheets
    - Flat sheets
    - Pillowcases
    - Pillows
    - Blankets
    - Mattress pad or cover
    - Bedspread or comforter

- Table linen
    - Napkins for eight

- Large formal tablecloth
- Napkins and plastic mats for informal use
- Cotton or pad liner for tablecloth
- Smaller tablecloths and napkins for "children's table"

- Bath linen
    - Four large bath towels
    - Matching hand towels

- Matching face cloths
- Midsize "hair towels" for women's hair
- Bath mat
- Shower curtain
- Small guest towels

🞰 Cookware
- Frying pan
- Covered saucepans (large and small)
- Tea kettle
- Utensil set
- Baking pans

🞰 China (formal service for eight, sometimes twelve, plus everyday service for eight)
- Dinner plates
- Salad plates
- Cups and saucers
- Creamer and sugar bowl
- Salt and pepper shakers
- Soup bowls
- Bread and butter plates

- Serving platters
- Glassware/crystal
- Water goblets
- Wine glasses
- Cocktail glasses
- Champagne glasses

🞰 Silverware (formal service for eight, sometimes twelve, plus everyday service for eight)
- Knives
- Dinner forks
- Salad forks
- Soup spoons
- Teaspoons

🞰 Silverware (additions to formal service)
- Butter knife
- Fish knife
- Dessert fork
- Shrimp fork
- Iced tea spoon
- Steak knife
- Specialized serving utensils (carving knife, slotted spoon, pie server, gravy boat and spoon, chafing dish)

While sheets, napkins and towels are important, newly-weds cannot live by linen alone. The following are some wedding gifts that have proved popular and well received in recent years. Any of the following items can be added to your bridal registry. Don't worry about the price tags, various guests can pitch in to buy you some of the more expensive items as a group gift.

- ℘ Videocassette recorder
- ℘ Camcorder
- ℘ Laser disc player
- ℘ Microwave oven
- ℘ Food processor
- ℘ CD-ROM drive for computer
- ℘ Fine cutlery
- ℘ High-end cookware
- ℘ Place settings (china, silver, crystal)
- ℘ Garage door opener
- ℘ Computer software
- ℘ Closet storage/shelving
- ℘ Carpeting (gift certificate), or fine rugs
- ℘ Floor or table lamp
- ℘ Clock radio
- ℘ Coffee maker

Here's a checklist of some of the items you might put on your registry.

Formal dinnerware (china):
(Specify manufacturer, pattern, quantity.)
- ☐ Dinner plates
- ☐ Salad/dessert plates
- ☐ Bread and butter plates
- ☐ Cups and saucers
- ☐ Rimmed soup bowls
- ☐ Soup/cereal bowls
- ☐ Open vegetable dishes
- ☐ Covered vegetable dishes
- ☐ Gravy boat
- ☐ Sugar bowl
- ☐ Creamer
- ☐ Small platter

- ☐ Medium platter
- ☐ Large platter
- ☐ Salt and pepper shakers
- ☐ Coffeepot
- ☐ Teapot
- ☐ Butter dish

Casual dinnerware:
(Specify manufacturer, pattern, quantity.)
- ☑ Dinner plates 24
- ☑ Salad/dessert plates 24
- ☐ Bread and butter plates
- ☑ Cups and saucers 24
- ☐ Rimmed soup bowls
- ☑ Soup/cereal bowls 24

- ☑ Open vegetable dishes
- ☑ Covered vegetable dishes
- ☐ Gravy boat
- ☐ Sugar bowl
- ☐ Creamer
- ☑ Small platter
- ☑ Medium platter
- ☑ Large platter
- ☑ Salt and pepper shakers
- ☐ Coffeepot
- ☑ Butter dish
- ☐ Mug

Formal flatware/ silverware:

(Specify manufacturer, pattern, quantity.)

- ☐ Four piece place setting
- ☐ Dinner forks
- ☐ Dinner knives
- ☐ Teaspoons
- ☐ Salad forks
- ☐ Soup spoons
- ☐ Butter spreader
- ☐ Butter knives
- ☐ Cold meat fork
- ☐ Sugar spoon
- ☐ Serving spoon
- ☐ Pierced spoon
- ☐ Gravy ladle
- ☐ Pie/cake server
- ☐ Hostess set
- ☐ Serve set
- ☐ Silver chest

Casual flatware:

(Specify manufacturer, pattern, quantity.)

- ☐ Dinner forks
- ☐ Dinner knives
- ☐ Teaspoons
- ☐ Salad forks
- ☐ Soup spoons
- ☐ Hostess set
- ☐ Serve set

Glassware:

(Specify manufacturer, pattern, quantity.)

- ☐ Goblets
- ☐ Wine glasses
- ☐ Champagne flutes
- ☐ Champagne saucers
- ☐ Old Fashioned glasses
- ☐ Highball glasses
- ☐ Iced beverage glasses
- ☐ Liqueur glasses
- ☐ Brandy snifters
- ☐ Hock wine glasses
- ☐ White wine glasses
- ☐ Double Old Fashioned glasses

Bar and glassware:

(Specify manufacturer, pattern, quantity.)

- ☐ Pilsner glasses
- ☐ Beer mugs
- ☐ Decanter
- ☐ Ice bucket
- ☐ Champagne cooler
- ☐ Whiskey set
- ☐ Martini set
- ☐ Wine rack

Holloware:

(Specify manufacturer, pattern, quantity.)

- [ ] Sugar/creamer
- [ ] Water pitcher
- [ ] Decanter
- [ ] Candlestick pair
- [ ] Coffee service
- [ ] Serving tray
- [ ] Relish tray
- [ ] Canape tray
- [ ] Chip-n-dip server
- [ ] Cheese board
- [ ] Cake plate
- [ ] Large salad bowl
- [ ] Salad bowl set
- [ ] Salad tongs
- [ ] Gravy boat
- [ ] Butter dish
- [ ] Salt and pepper shakers
- [ ] Round baker
- [ ] Rectangular baker
- [ ] Duo server
- [ ] Punch bowl set
- [ ] Demitasse set

(With many of the above items you will be asked to specify whether you want them in crystal, brass, wood, ceramic, glass, or some other make.)

Gifts/home decor items:

- [ ] Vase
- [ ] Bud vase
- [ ] Bowl
- [ ] Candlestick pair
- [ ] Picture frame
- [ ] Figurine
- [ ] Clock
- [ ] Lamp
- [ ] Framed art

- [ ] Brass accessories
- [ ] Picnic basket

Small electric appliances:

- [ ] Coffee maker ✓
- [ ] Coffee grinder ✓
- [ ] Espresso/ cappuccino maker
- [x] Food processor
- [ ] Mini processor
- [ ] Mini chopper
- [ ] Blender
- [ ] Hand mixer
- [ ] Stand mixer
- [ ] Bread baker
- [ ] Pasta machine
- [x] Citrus juicer
- [ ] Juice extractor
- [ ] Toaster (specify two-slice or four-slice)
- [x] Toaster oven
- [ ] Convection oven
- [ ] Microwave
- [ ] Electric fry pan
- [ ] Electric wok
- [ ] Electric griddle
- [ ] Sandwich maker
- [ ] Waffle maker
- [ ] Hot tray
- [ ] Indoor grill
- [ ] Crock pot
- [ ] Rice cooker
- [ ] Can opener
- [ ] Food slicer
- [ ] Electric knife
- [x] Iron / BOARD
- [ ] Vacuum
- [ ] Fan

- [ ] Humidifier ✓
- [ ] Dehumidifier
- [ ] Heater ✓

Cutlery:
- [ ] Carving set ✓
  (specify quantity)
- [ ] Cutlery set ✓
  (specify quantity)
- [ ] Knife set (specify quantity) ✓
- [ ] Knife block ✓
- [ ] Steel sharpener ✓
- [ ] Boning knife (specify size)
- [ ] Paring knife (specify size) ✓
- [ ] Chef knife (specify size)
- [ ] Bread knife (specify size)
- [ ] Slicing knife (specify size)
- [ ] Carving fork
- [ ] Utility knife (specify size)
- [ ] Kitchen shears
- [ ] Cleaver

Bakeware:
- [ ] Cake pan
- [ ] Cookie sheet
- [ ] Bread pan
- [ ] Muffin tin
- [ ] Cooling rack
- [ ] Bundt pan
- [ ] Spring form cake pan
- [ ] Pie plate
- [ ] Roasting pan
- [ ] Pizza pan
- [ ] Covered casserole
- [ ] Soufflé dish
- [ ] Rectangular baker
- [ ] Lasagna pan
- [ ] Pizza pan

Kitchen basics:
- [ ] Kitchen tool set
- [ ] Canister set
- [ ] Spice rack
- [ ] Cutting board
- [ ] Salad bowl set
- [ ] Salt and pepper mill
- [ ] Kitchen towel
- [ ] Pot holders
- [ ] Apron
- [ ] Mixing bowl set
- [ ] Measuring cup set
- [ ] Rolling pin
- [ ] Cookie jar
- [ ] Tea kettle
- [ ] Coffee mugs

Cookware:
- [ ] Saucepan (small)
- [ ] Saucepan (medium)
- [ ] Saucepan (large)
- [ ] Sauté pan (small)
- [ ] Sauté pan (large)
- [ ] Frypan (small)
- [ ] Frypan (medium)
- [ ] Frypan (large)
- [ ] Stockpot (small)
- [ ] Stockpot (large)
- [ ] Roast pan
- [ ] Omelette pan (small)
- [ ] Omelette pan (large)
- [ ] Skillet
- [ ] Double boiler
- [ ] Steamer insert
- [ ] Wok
- [ ] Griddle
- [ ] Stirfry
- [ ] Microwave cookware set
- [ ] Tea kettle
- [ ] Dutch oven

☑ Air Purifier
☑ Juicer

Luggage:
- ☐ Duffel
- ☐ Beauty case
- ☐ Carry-on tote
- ☑ Pullman bags (specify quantity and sizes)
- ☐ Garment bag
- ☐ Luggage cart

Home electronics:
- ☐ Stereo
- ☐ CD player
- ☐ Television
- ☐ VCR
- ☐ Video camera
- ☐ Telephone
- ☐ Answering machine
- ☐ Computer or word processor
- ☐ Portable stereo
- ☑ Camera
- ✓ computer

Ready-to-assemble:
- ☐ Chair
- ☐ Stool
- ☐ Snack table
- ☐ Dining set (specify quantity of seats)
- ☐ Entertainment center

Formal table linens:
(Specify color theme.)
- ☐ Tablecloth
- ☐ Place mats
- ☐ Napkins
- ☐ Napkin rings

Casual table linens:
(Specify color theme.)
- ☐ Tablecloth
- ☐ Place mats
- ☐ Napkins
- ☐ Napkin rings

Master bed:
(Specify color theme and bed size.)
- ☑ Flat sheet
- ☑ Fitted sheet
- ☑ Pillowcase
- ☑ Set of sheets
- ☑ Comforter
- ☐ Comforter set
- ☑ Dust ruffle
- ☐ Pillow sham
- ☐ Window treatment
- ☐ Down comforter
- ☑ Duvet cover
- ☐ Bedspread
- ☐ Quilt
- ☐ Blanket
- ☐ Electric blanket
- ☐ Cotton blanket
- ☐ Decorative pillows
- ☐ Down pillow (specify Standard, Queen, or King)
- ☐ Pillow (specify Standard, Queen, or King)
- ☑ Mattress pad

Guest bed:
(Specify color and bed size.)
- ☐ Flat sheet
- ☐ Fitted sheet
- ☐ Pillowcase

- [ ] Set of sheets
- [ ] Comforter
- [ ] Comforter set
- [ ] Dust ruffle
- [ ] Pillow sham
- [ ] Window treatment
- [ ] Down comforter
- [ ] Duvet cover
- [ ] Bedspread
- [ ] Quilt
- [ ] Blanket
- [ ] Electric blanket
- [ ] Cotton blanket
- [ ] Decorative pillow
- [ ] Down pillow (specify Standard, Queen, or King)
- [ ] Pillow (specify Standard, Queen, or King)
- [ ] Mattress pad

Master bath:
(Specify colors.)
- [x] Bath towel
- [x] Hand towel
- [x] Washcloth
- [x] Fingertip towel
- [ ] Body sheet
- [ ] Shower curtain
- [ ] Bath mat
- [ ] Bath rug
- [ ] Lid cover
- [ ] Hamper
- [ ] Scale
- [ ] Wastebasket

Guest bath:
(Specify colors.)
- [ ] Bath towel
- [ ] Hand towel
- [ ] Washcloth
- [ ] Fingertip towel
- [ ] Body sheet
- [ ] Shower curtain
- [ ] Bath mat
- [ ] Bath rug
- [ ] Lid cover
- [ ] Hamper
- [ ] Scale
- [ ] Waste basket

Grooming aids for the bride:
- [ ] Fragrance
- [ ] Perfume
- [ ] Cologne
- [ ] Body lotion
- [ ] Powder
- [ ] Body cream

Grooming aids for the groom:
- [ ] Cologne
- [ ] After-shave
- [ ] After-shave balm

Intimates:
- [ ] Peignoir set
- [ ] Short gown
- [ ] Long gown
- [ ] Camisole
- [ ] Tap pant
- [ ] Teddy

CHAPTER FIVE

Party Time: Bridal Showers

*M*ost of us know that a bridal shower is not where the members of the bridal party stand in the tub and take turns soaping up under the shower head. The typical shower is held either at a small function hall or in someone's home, depending on the size of the guest list. The guests are women only, but your fiancé usually comes along for the ride, for no reason other than to sit around looking awkward as you unwrap one gift after the next.

Once upon a time, it was customary to keep the specifics of the shower—time, date, location, and so on—a secret from the bride until the last possible moment. These days, however, it is more and more common for the bride to take an active part in planning the festivities.

The Guest List

You don't have to invite all the women who'll be at the wedding to your shower. Usually, bridal showers are much more about intimate get-togethers than grandiose affairs. You, your wedding attendants, family members, and 5 to 30 of your closest friends should make the party a success story.

Shower Menu Suggestions

For a breakfast shower:

- Bagels
- Croissants
- Muffins
- Doughnuts
- Coffee cake
- Juices
- Mimosas
- Fresh fruit
- Omelettes
- Belgian waffles
- French toast
- Pancakes
- Bacon
- Sausage
- Ham

Bridal Shower Checklist

RSVP	NAME	ADDRESS
❑	1.	
❑	2.	
❑	3.	
❑	4.	
❑	5.	
❑	6.	
❑	7.	
❑	8.	
❑	9.	
❑	10.	
❑	11.	
❑	12.	
❑	13.	
❑	14.	
❑	15.	
❑	16.	
❑	17.	
❑	18.	
❑	19.	
❑	20.	
❑	21.	
❑	22.	
❑	23.	
❑	24.	
❑	25.	

RSVP	NAME	ADDRESS
❏	26.	
❏	27.	
❏	28.	
❏	29.	
❏	30.	
❏	31.	
❏	32.	
❏	33.	
❏	34.	
❏	35.	
❏	36.	
❏	37.	
❏	38.	
❏	39.	
❏	40.	
❏	41.	
❏	42.	
❏	43.	
❏	44.	
❏	45.	
❏	46.	
❏	47.	
❏	48.	
❏	49.	
❏	50.	

For an afternoon shower:

- Cold-cut platters
- Tuna salad with rolls
- Seafood salad with rolls
- Pasta salad
- Garden salad
- Potato salad
- Macaroni salad
- Swedish meatballs
- Soda
- Punch

Appetizers:

- Calzone (rolled pizza)
- Fried chicken wings
- Stuffed mushrooms
- Crab cakes
- Zucchini appetizers

- Meatballs
- Beef teriyaki strips
- Shrimp cocktail
- Scallops
- Chicken fingers
- Vegetable platter with dip

Desserts:

- Brownies
- Blondies
- Pistachio surprise bars
- Frosted pumpkin bars
- Dutch apple cake
- Raspberry squares
- Lemon squares
- Congo bars
- Chocolate-dipped strawberries
- Shower cake

The Gift Recorder

The most important thing to remember for any shower is to assign someone the task of keeping track of your gifts. If you're in on the planning, bring this book with you and assign someone you trust with the task of filling out the following recorder. This way, you'll know who gave you which gift when the time comes to send out the thank-you notes.

Gift Checklist

NAME	DESCRIPTION OF GIFT	THANK-YOU NOTE SENT?
1.		❑
2.		❑
3.		❑
4.		❑
5.		❑
6.		❑
7.		❑
8.		❑
9.		❑
10.		❑
11.		❑
12.		❑
13.		❑
14.		❑
15.		❑
16.		❑
17.		❑
18.		❑
19.		❑
20.		❑
21.		❑
22.		❑
23.		❑
24.		❑
25.		❑

Let the Games Begin

Nothing kinky here. These are just a way to liven things up a bit for your guests.

🎀 Guess the Goodies—Fill a large decorative jar with white or colored candied almonds. Ask the guests to figure out how many almonds are in the jar. They can take as long as they want to hazard a guess; at the end of the shower, they hand in their answers on a slip of paper. The person who comes closest to the number wins the jar and the almonds. (Feel free to substitute chocolate kisses, M&M's, jelly beans, or anything else you can think of.)

🎀 Mish-Mash Marriage—Scramble the letter in words associated with love and marriage: kiss (siks), love (voel), garter (tergar), and so on. Set a time limit for the guests to figure out the scrambles; the one who completes the most gets a prize.

🎀 Mystery Spices—Find 10 jars filled with different spices. Place masking tape over the labels; spread the jars out on a table and let the guests try to guess what's in each jar. They may shake, examine, and even open and sniff the contents—just as long as they don't read the labels. Set a time limit, and when it's up, the spices can go to the person who correctly guessed the identity of the most jars.

🎀 Bride's Chatter—Assign someone to keep a record of the bride's comments while she's opening her gifts. After she's through, read the comments back to the group. Taken out of context, the remarks are sometimes hilarious.

🎀 Famous Couple Trivia—Trivia is all the rage these days, so why not develop some trivia questions with a love theme for your shower? This could be your very own version of *Who Wants to Be a Millionaire*. Given the nature of your prizes, however, it might be more appropriate to name it "Who Wants to Win a Bar of Fancy Soap." Sample questions can be:

• What famous singing TV couple of the 70s had their own show? (Hint: "I've Got You, Babe") (Answer: Sonny and Cher)

• What was Roy Rogers's wife's name? (Hint: It wasn't Trigger) (Answer: Dale Evans)

• Who were Lucy and Ricky Ricardo's best friends? (Answer: Fred and Ethel Mertz)

୫୫ Memory Game—After the bride-to-be has opened all of her gifts, she is asked to leave the room for a few minutes. Once she's left the room, pass out pencils and paper to the guests and ask them to answer questions about the guest-of-honor: What is she wearing? What color are her shoes? Does she have nail polish on? Is she wearing earrings? What is her middle name? And any other questions you can think of. The guest with the most correct answers wins a prize.

୫୫ Right Date Door Prize—Ask all of the guests for the date of their wedding anniversary (or birthday for single guests). Whoever has a date that comes closest to the wedding date wins a prize.

୫୫ Bride's Bingo—This game can be bought at most stationery and card stores. Bride's Bingo is the same concept as regular bingo, only words associated with weddings replace those boring numbers.

୫୫ Pin It on the Groom—If your live groom is unwilling to volunteer his services, draw the silhouette of a man on a large piece of paper. Attach a photo of the groom's face to the top. Blindfold the guests, spin them, and have them attempt to pin a flower on his lapel.

CHAPTER SIX

Wedding Consultants

$\mathcal{M}$ ost women today are busy juggling the dual demands of private life and a career. Add the daunting proposition of planning a wedding, and some women may find themselves getting a little, well, frenzied. Even if you have tons of spare time on your hands, you may still want someone to show you the ropes when it comes to planning your wedding. That's where wedding consultants come in. Whether you want someone to take you by the hand and do everything for you or you just need a little advice on a few key issues, there's someone out there to help you. Of course, you'll have to pay a bit for the help, but the advice and services you will get (and the aggravation they will avoid) may be worth the dough.

Independent Consultants

Weddings are the first and only business of independent consultants. If you wish, they will handle the whole wedding for you: flowers, food, photography, caterer, reception site, music, and everything else. The consultant can even serve as the master of ceremonies at the reception.

Costs for this kind of consultant can vary. Some charge a flat rate; others ask for anywhere from 10 to 20 percent of the total cost of the wedding. That can add up in a hurry, but to some brides, the experience and industry contacts of these consultants are worth the expense. (Note: Though these consultants will probably offer to coordinate your whole wedding, you should feel free to confine their role to the few areas you feel you need help in, if that's the way you'd prefer to go.)

Store-Affiliated Consultants

These consultants are employed by bridal salons, reception sites, and other businesses that cater to weddings. Their knowledge is usually limited to a particular area of exper-tise—but it does have the advantage of being free, provided you give your business to the establishment that employs the consultant.

Picking the Right Person

How should you go about picking the right consultant for you? As far as store-affiliated consultants go, you can't. You get whoever is employed by the store and available at the time you come in. You have no real choice—other than to shop somewhere else. With an independent consultant, on the other hand, you will want to select someone who listens to your needs and ideas, and who you feel is capable of handling the job. Ask friends, family, and coworkers for referrals. If they all come up empty, consult the local phone book and ask people in the industry, such as florists, photographers, and bridal shops. Below is a list of questions that should help you find the right indepen-dent consultant for you.

- 🕭 How long has the consultant been in business? (Many years in business means lots of experience and contacts. It also means that a consultant is probably reputable, as he or she hasn't been run out of town by dissatisfied customers.)
- 🕭 Is the consultant full-time or part-time?
- 🕭 Can you get references from former customers?
- 🕭 Is the consultant a full-service planner, or does his or her expertise lie only in certain areas?
- 🕭 If the consultant isn't a full-service planner, what services does he or she handle?
- 🕭 What organizations is the consultant affiliated with?
- 🕭 Is the consultant scheduled to work with any other weddings that are on the same day as yours?

(You don't want your consultant to be too busy
with someone else to meet your needs.)

- ❦ How much (or how little) of the consultant's time
will be devoted to your wedding?
- ❦ What is the cost? How is it computed? (Hourly?
By percentage? A flat fee?)
- ❦ If the consultant works on a percentage basis,
how is the final cost determined?
- ❦ Exactly what does the quoted fee include (or omit)?

Name: _____

Address: _____

Phone: _____

Contact: _____

Hours: _____

Appointments: _____

Date: _____ Time: _____

Date: _____ Time: _____

Date: _____ Time: _____

Service: _____

Number of hours: _____

Overtime cost: _____

Provides the following services: _____

_____

_____

Cost: _____

Fee: Flat:_____ Hourly percentage: _____ Per guest: _____

Total amount due: _____

Amount of deposit: _____ Date: _____

Amount due: _____ Date: _____

Gratuities included?   Yes   No

Sales tax included?   Yes   No

Date contract signed: _____

Terms of cancellation: _____

CHAPTER SEVEN

The Ceremony

S quaring away the details of your ceremony should be one of your first and highest priorities. If you don't know the time and date of the ceremony, then you certainly can't do much reception planning.

As for the kind of ceremony you'll have, you should first decide whether it's going to be religiously-based or a civil act.

(Note: Marriage requirements and specific ceremony rites will vary from religion to religion. If you are interested in having a religious ceremony, consult with your officiant as soon as possible to learn what restrictions and guidelines will apply.) If you decide on a civil ceremony, don't feel tied to the old stereotype of a quick, drab exchange of "I do's" in a judge's chambers. With the exception of a religious site, you can have your civil ceremony anywhere you wish—and make it as beautiful and spirited as you've ever dreamed.

It's advisable to set a ceremony date 6 to 12 months before you want the wedding to occur, particularly if you want a date during the peak time between April and October. Competition for ceremony sites in those months can be pretty fierce, so you're more likely to get the day and time you want if you start looking early. If you don't plan on having that long an engagement, the best rule to follow is to arrange the date as soon as you possibly can.

When you meet with your ceremony officiant to discuss a wedding date, make sure to have a list of questions ready for him or her to answer. You should also find out what you will be required to do. Here is a list of potential questions you might ask:

- ☐ Are there any restrictions placed on your ability to marry?
- ☐ What is the procedure for an interfaith marriage?
- ☐ Are there any papers to be filled out, bans to be posted?
- ☐ Are there any premarital counseling requirements? If so, what are they?
- ☐ What does the ceremony consist of?
- ☐ Will you be permitted to write your own vows?
- ☐ What kind of services does the facility provide (music, reception area)?
- ☐ What fees are required for marrying in the facility? What are the costs?
- ☐ What do the fees include?
- ☐ Can you include family members and close friends in the ceremony as readers, candle lighters, singers, and such?
- ☐ Will the facility provide any decorations? Carpeting? Aisle runner? Ribbon?
- ☐ Are there any restrictions as to the kind of music you can have at the ceremony?
- ☐ What are the rules regarding photography and video recording?
- ☐ Will you be dealing with a coordinator for the ceremony site over the course of planning the ceremony, or speaking directly with the officiant?
- ☐ Do you have facilities for the bridal party to wait and freshen up in while they wait for the ceremony to begin?
- ☐ Are there any other weddings that day?
- ☐ What about custodial services after the wedding?
- ☐ Is there room to have a receiving line at the back of the facility? What about outside, in a courtyard or garden?
- ☐ What is the parking situation?

Ceremony site: _____
Address: _____
_____
_____
Officiant name: _____
Phone number: _____
Additional meetings/premarital counseling sessions
Place: _____ Date: _____ Time: _____

Licensed to Wed

What do driving, fishing, hunting, boating, selling alcohol, and getting married all have in common? Legally, you need a license for every one of them. Admittedly, you're not threatening the public safety by getting married (unless you're planning a particularly festive reception), but that license binds you as a couple in the eyes of the law. As an added bonus, the blood test required to get the license helps you make sure you're not mistakenly marrying your long-lost brother or any other closer-than-they-should-be relations.

While the criteria required to get a marriage license varies from state to state—and you should definitely contact your local marriage bureau (usually at the City Clerk's office) to find out exactly what you'll need to do—the following license requirements are common to all states:

- You and your groom must apply for your license together.
- You must both have all of the required paperwork:
  - Birth certificates
  - Driver's licenses
  - Proof of age
  - Proof of citizenship

- You both need completed blood tests and doctor's certificates from both doctors.
- You must provide proof of divorce or annulment (in the case of a previous marriage).
- You must pay a fee. The fee usually ranges from $10 to $30.
- Plan on dragging your best man and maid of honor along when it comes time to sign the license. They need to be there as witnesses, to prove that you weren't harassed into the institution of marriage.

Different Strokes

If you decide on a religious ceremony, consult with your officiant about premarital requirements. Religions differ in their rules and restrictions, as do different branches within the same religion. Your first meeting with the officiant should clear up most of the technical details and give you the opportunity to ask questions.

Although religions differ too much to make a blanket statement about each one's approach to the marriage rite, the following should give you a general idea about what to expect from some of the major religions' ceremonies.

Roman Catholic Ceremony and Preparations

If you're getting married within the Catholic Church, you're probably aware that you're up against some hefty premarital requirements. The following are the most significant (read "time-consuming"):

- Technically, it is impossible to remarry within the Catholic Church if your first spouse is still alive. A civil divorce will not do the trick; you must receive an annulment. It's a long process, so it's smart to get the ball rolling at least a year before you plan to wed.

🪝 Premarital counseling, also known as "Pre-Cana" (premarriage), is required by the Catholic Church. Expect a lot of talking between you, your groom, and your priest about your religious convictions and important marriage issues; workshops with other engaged couples; and even some compatibility quizzes. If you need to pursue counseling, sign up ASAP, because space is limited.

🪝 As far as the ceremony itself, you'll be glad to know that contrary to popular belief, the Catholic ceremony does not go on and on and on. Although you have the option of incorporating a complete Mass (which adds about 15 minutes to the total time), this is not a requirement. From the moment the organ announces your arrival at the altar to the time you walk back down the aisle with your new husband, approximately half an hour will have elapsed. So what is going on?

- Introductory Rites. The ceremony starts with opening music selections; once you reach the altar, the priest greets you and your guests, offers Penitential rites, and says an opening prayer.
- Liturgy of the Word. This is when the reading you have chosen will be read, perhaps by special friends or family members. At the completion of the reading, the priest gives a brief homily that focuses on some aspect of marriage.

- Rite of Marriage. Here's where you see some action. After the declaration of consent, the rings are blessed and exchanged. What most people don't realize is that the exchange of vows, not the ring exchange, is the act that marks the official moment of marriage.

The Protestant Ceremony and Preparations

Protestant marriages of all denominations have far fewer requirements and restrictions than Catholic marriages. An informational meeting with the clergy is required, but pre-marital counseling is optional. Furthermore, there is no need for an annulment if either party has been divorced.

The Protestant religion encompasses a great many denominations, but the basic elements of the marriage ceremony are the same. Here's a brief overview of what to expect:

- The ceremony begins; members of the wedding party walk up the aisle.
- The couple welcome their guests.
- A Prayer of Blessing is said.
- Scripture passages are read.
- There is a Giving in Marriage (affirmation by parents).
- The congregation gives its response.
- Vows and rings are exchanged.
- The celebration of the Lord's Supper takes place.
- The unity candle is lit.
- The Benediction is given.
- The Recessional takes place.

Jewish Ceremonies and Preparations

Judaism, too, has different "divisions" that
adhere to different rules; however, in the
Orthodox, Conservative, and Reform traditions, certain elements of the wedding
ceremony are basically the same.

- The marriage ceremony is conducted under a
  huppah, an ornamented canopy (optional in the
  Reform ceremony).
- The Seven Blessings are recited.
- The bride and groom drink blessed wine; the
  groom then smashes the glass with his foot. Don't
  worry; the glass is wrapped in a napkin to prevent
  flying shards from landing in someone's eye or
  from harming the groom's foot.
- The newly married couple is toasted with the
  expression "Mazel tov!" ("Good luck!").

Jewish marriages within the more stringent Orthodox
and Conservative branches have a few stipulations that are
rigidly adhered to. They are:

- Weddings cannot take place on the Sabbath
  or any time that is considered holy.
- Ceremonies are performed in Hebrew or
  Aramaic only.
- No interfaith marriages are to be conducted.
- Men must wear yarmulkes.
- Bride wears her wedding ring on her right hand.

While Reform ceremonies also cannot take place on
the Sabbath or any other holy time, they do differ from
Orthodox and Conservative ceremonies in a few ways.

🪶 Bride wears her ring on her left hand.

🪶 In English-speaking countries, the ceremony is performed in both English and Hebrew.

🪶 Note: Preparations for ceremonies differ depending on the tradition. Check with your rabbi for specific details.

If Yours Is an Interfaith Marriage . . .

If you're marrying outside your religion, you might run up against certain obstacles. Then again, things might go smoother than you'd have expected. Here are a few of the ground rules for interfaith marriages:

🪶 The Catholic Church will sanction a marriage between a Catholic and a non-Catholic providing all of the Church's concerns are met. Contrary to popular belief, it is not necessary for, say, a Jewish person to convert to Catholicism in order to marry in a Catholic ceremony.

🪶 In marriages between a Protestant and a Catholic, officiants from both religions may take part in the ceremony if the couple wishes.

🪶 In a Jewish-Christian wedding, even the most liberal clergy will rarely perform a joint ceremony in the temple or church. These ceremonies usually take place at the actual reception site.

Your Wedding Vows

If you're perfectly satisfied with the traditional civil or religious vows, go ahead and skip on to the next chapter—individualized vows aren't for everyone. However, if you're looking for something different to say at the altar, an alternative to the traditional wedding vows, look no further. The list of questions contained within this chapter is designed to get you on the road to finding the perfect vow for you and your fiancé.

When creating your own vows, start by writing down answers to the following questions. Doing so will provide you with valuable source material, and help you develop the vows you're looking for.

Answer together: How do you, as a couple, define the following terms?

Love: _____

_____

_____

Trust: _____

_____

_____

Marriage: _____

_____

_____

Family: _____

_____

_____

Commitment: _____

_____

_____

Togetherness: _____

_____

_____

Answer together: How did the two of you first meet?

_____

_____

_____

*Answer separately: What was the first thing you
noticed about your partner?*

Bride: _____

_____

_____

Groom: _____

_____

_____

*Answer together: List here any shared hobbies or
other mutual interests you share.*

_____

_____

_____

*Answer together: What was the single most impor-
tant event in your relationship? (Or, what was the event
that you feel says the most about your development as
a couple?)*

_____

_____

_____

*Answer together: How similar (or different) were your
respective childhoods? Take a moment and try to recount
some of the important parallels or differences here.*

_____

_____

_____

Answer together: Is there a song, poem or book that is particularly meaningful in your relationship? If so, identify it here.

_____
_____
_____

Answer together: Do you and your partner share a common religious tradition? If so, identify it here.

_____
_____
_____

Answer together: If you share a common religious tradition, is there a particular scriptural passage that you as a couple find particularly meaningful? If so, identify it here.

_____
_____
_____

Answer together: Why did your parents' marriages succeed or fail? What marital pitfalls do you want to avoid? What can you take from your parents' examples, good or bad?

_____
_____
_____

Answer together: Take some time to reminisce about the course of your relationship. When did you first realize you loved each other? When did you first say the words? What trials and tribulations has your love had to overcome? What shared memories are you most fond of?

_____
_____
_____

Answer separately: What do you love about your partner? Why?

Bride:_____

_____

_____

Groom:_____

_____

_____

Answer together: How do you and your partner look at personal growth and change? What aspects of your life together are likely to change over the coming years? How do you anticipate dealing with those changes? How important is mutual respect and tolerance in your relationship? When one of you feels that a particular need is being overlooked, what do you feel is the best way to address this problem with the other person?

_____

_____

_____

_____

_____

Answer together: Do you and your partner have a common vision of what your life as older people will be like? Will it include children or grandchildren? Take this opportunity to put into words the vision you and your partner share of what it will be like to grow old together.

_____

_____

_____

_____

_____

Great Names in Romantic Writing

For extra inspiration, you might want to consult the masters of the written word. The following wordsmiths have a lot to offer a bride and groom in the way of wedding vows and supplementary reading material.

- Maya Angelou
- Anne Bradstreet
- Elizabeth Barrett Browning
- Willa Cather
- e.e. cummings
- Emily Dickinson
- John Donne
- Ralph Waldo Emerson
- Ben Jonson
- John Keats
- Anne Morrow Lindbergh
- Henry Wadsworth Longfellow
- John Milton
- William Shakespeare
- Percy Bysshe Shelley
- Virgil
- William Carlos Williams

First Draft of Our Wedding Vow

_____

_____

_____

_____

_____

_____

_____

_____

_____

_____

_____

_____

_____

_____

_____

_____

_____

_____

_____

_____

_____

_____

_____

_____

_____

_____

_____

_____

_____

_____

_____

_____

_____

Second Draft of Our Wedding Vow

_____
_____
_____
_____
_____
_____
_____
_____
_____
_____
_____
_____
_____
_____
_____
_____
_____
_____
_____
_____
_____
_____
_____
_____
_____
_____
_____
_____
_____
_____
_____
_____
_____

CHAPTER EIGHT

Ceremony Music

B efore you begin to pick out music for your wedding ceremony, be sure to check with the officiant of your house of worship for guidelines. There always seem to be new policies on what selections are appropriate in a religious setting; what was forbidden last year may be accepted next month. It's a good idea to find out what you can and can't use before you get your heart set on something.

You should also . . .

- ☐ Meet with the musical director from your house of worship to discuss appropriate selections.
- ☐ Discuss fees for the organist and any additional musicians that may be provided.
- ☐ Begin to choose the selection for each distinct part of the ceremony at least two months before the wedding.

The Prelude

The prelude sets the mood . . . and provides a little listening enjoyment for your guests while they await your arrival.

Selections

_____

_____

At the conclusion of the prelude, the mother of the bride is seated. This is a good time to feature a song with a vocalist.

Selections

_____

_____

The Processional

The processional is played as the wedding party makes its way down the aisle. When the bride begins her march down, something selected especially for her is played. (An alternative, however, is for the bride to walk down the aisle to the same tune as the rest of the party, played at a different tempo.)

Some processional favorites (and their composers) include:

- "Waltz of the Flowers," Tchaikovsky
- "Wedding March," Mendelssohn
- Bridal Chorus ("Here Comes the Bride"), Wagner
- "Trumpet Voluntary," Dupuis
- "Trumpet Voluntary," Clarke
- "Trumpet Tune," Purcell
- "The Dance of the Sugar Plum Fairies," Tchaikovsky
- "Ode to Joy," Beethoven
- "The March," Tchaikovsky
- "Ave Maria," Schubert
- "The Austrian Wedding March," traditional

Selections

_____

_____

The Ceremony

During the ceremony itself, you may wish to hear songs that have a special meaning for you and your groom. If nothing comes to mind, ask your officiant for ideas. He or she will probably be able to suggest dozens of wonderful songs that can add meaning to what's taking place.

Some ceremony music favorites (and their composers) include:

- "My Tribute," Crouch
- "The Lord's Prayer," Malotte
- "Panis Angelicus," Franck
- "Now Thank We All Our God," Bach
- "Cherish the Treasure," Mohr
- "We've Only Just Begun," The Carpenters
- "The Unity Candle Song," Sullivan
- "The Bride's Prayer," Good
- "The Wedding Prayer," Dunlap
- "Wherever You Go," Callahan
- "The Wedding Song," Paul Stookey
- "The Irish Wedding Song," traditional

Selections

_____

_____

The Recessional

The recessional is played at the conclusion of the ceremony as the members of the wedding party make their way back down the aisle. It's usually an upbeat and joyful selection, one that echoes the feelings of the newly joined couple.

Some recessional favorites (and their composers) include:

- "The Russian Dance," Tchaikovsky
- "Trumpet Tune," Stanley
- "Toccata Symphony V," Widor
- "All Creatures of Our God and King," Williams
- "Trumpet Fanfare (Rondeau)," Mouret
- "Pomp and Circumstance," Elgar
- "Praise, My Soul, the King of Heaven," Goss

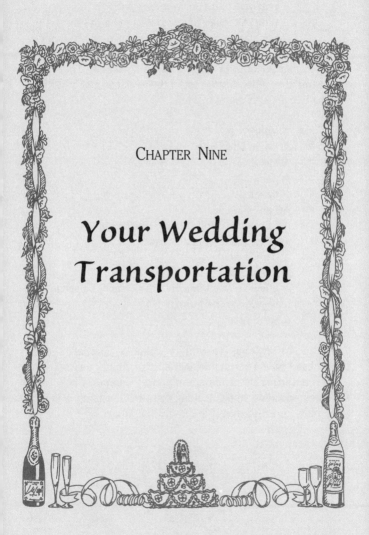

CHAPTER NINE

Your Wedding Transportation

*A*lmost anything that moves can be used to transport you and your wedding party to the wedding. Although limousines are still the most popular mode of wedding transportation, don't overlook the possibility of dropping down to the ceremony in a hot-air balloon, or floating up on a sailboat. There are dozens of options. If the cost of the rental would fit into your budget, why not consider . . .

- A trolley car
- A horse and buggy
- A sleigh
- A plane
- A glider
- An antique car
- An Excaliber, Rolls-Royce, Bentley, or another make of luxury car
- A parade float
- A motorcycle
- A unicycle (well, maybe not—it might be tough to maneuver in the gown)
- A speedboat

. . . or anything else you can think of. Granted, some of these options aren't practical all year round, and others can be a logistical nightmare—not every ceremony site comes equipped with a landing strip—but the point is you do have choices beyond the traditional limousine.

Of course, whatever means of transportation you decide on for your wedding day should fit into your budget. To ensure that you'll be getting quality transportation for your money, you should ask certain questions of any company you rent transportation from.

(Note: the following list of questions is geared toward limousine rental, but it will give you an idea of the kind of information you should get from any transportation supplier.)

- How long has the company been in business?
- Does the company have the proper license and insurance?
- Can you get references from former customers?
- Does the company own its vehicles? (Companies that don't own their own vehicles may have a hard time guaranteeing availability. They are also less likely to be on top of any mechanical problems or other unforeseen dilemmas.)
- Can you inspect the vehicles? (Check for cleanliness, dents, rust, and so on.)
- Does the company have the kind of vehicle you want? Will it be available on your wedding day?
- What are the rates? (Most limousine services charge by the hour. Unfortunately for you, the clock starts ticking the minute they leave their home base rather than when you start using the vehicle.)
- What is the company's cancellation policy?
- Is there a required minimum fee or number of rental hours?
- What is the policy on tipping? Is it included in the hourly rate, or should you account for it separately? (You won't want to tip your chauffeur at the end of the night if the gratuity is covered in the fee you paid. It's doubtful the service will be so spectacular that you'll want to pay twice!)

- 🪢 How much of a deposit is required to reserve the vehicle(s) for your wedding? When is the final payment due?
- 🪢 Will the company provide champagne? Ice? Glasses? A television? Will these items cost extra?
- 🪢 Before you give anyone your business, make sure you can get a written contract stipulating the date, time, type of vehicle, services, and costs.

Company name:_____

Phone:_____

Contact person:_____

Phone:_____

Type of vehicle:_____

Number of people vehicle holds:_____

Rental includes:_____

_____

Rate (overtime also):_____

Cancellation policy:_____

Deposit required:_____

Balance due: _____

If you're not renting transportation, but, say, borrowing a nice luxury car from a family member or friend, make sure the car is tuned up, cleaned, and filled with gas. (You should offer to pay for the car wash and fill the tank with gas before and after the wedding.)

What about Us?

You are also responsible for providing or arranging transportation for the members of your wedding party. You might also want to make sure your parents and the groom's parents won't be standing on the corner waiting for a bus to the ceremony. If your budget allows, consider renting an extra limousine or two to chauffeur them to and from the ceremony and reception sites. Otherwise arrange for those with the nicest cars to transport the rest of the group. Make sure everyone is aware of who's taking whom, what time people will have to be ready, and where they may have to meet.

The Going-Away Car

The odds are good that your attendants will try to trash your going-away car. For safety's sake, make sure they don't obstruct the view or movement of the driver. Any writing should be applied with washable shoe polish.

If you're lucky, your budget will allow you to keep your limousine (or other rented transportation) until the end of the reception. As your attendants may not be too keen to trash a rented luxury car, you can whip over to your hotel (or to the airport) in style and not have to worry about cans clanging behind you all the way.

Company name:_____

Phone:_____

Contact person:_____

Phone:_____

Type of vehicle:_____

Number of people vehicle holds:_____

Rental includes:_____

_____

Rate (overtime also):_____

Cancellation policy:_____

Deposit required: _____

Balance due: _____

CHAPTER TEN

The Wedding Rehearsal and Rehearsal Dinner

The purpose of the wedding rehearsal is to acquaint everyone in the wedding with the basics of the ceremony. Who (besides you and your groom) should attend? The officiant, every member of the wedding party, the father of the bride (to practice dragging her down the aisle, of course), any scripture readers and candle lighters, and any children taking part in the ceremony. Invite the florist to discuss any final issues of flower placement. You might also want to arrange for any featured soloists or musicians to attend the rehearsal as well. Remember, this will be your only chance to iron out any last-minute details and resolve any remaining questions. Though it may not be enough to truly calm your nerves, getting everything straight at the rehearsal is your last chance to make sure that everything is ready and all of the participants know what's expected of them.

The rehearsal is held at the ceremony site itself, usually on the night before the wedding. If that time is inconvenient for any of your key players, however, reschedule for another time, preferably during the week before the wedding. (If it's too far before the wedding, people may forget what they learned).

Rehearsal location: _____

Address: _____

Officiant: _____

Phone: _____

Date: _____ Time: _____

After your officiant meets the wedding party, he or she will give a quick overview of what will happen in the ceremony and who should be doing what. A quick practice run-through of the ceremony is next, and that's it. If only the real ceremony could be that easy!

The ceremony test run should include whichever are applicable of the following:

- Processional
- Opening words
- Giving away or blessing
- Reading
- Prayers
- Marriage vows
- Exchange of rings
- Pronouncement of marriage
- Lighting of unity candle
- Benediction
- Closing words
- Recessional

You might want to bring any essential items that you'll need for the wedding to the rehearsal. This way, you won't have to worry about carrying them with you in the limo ride to the ceremony.

- ☐ Wedding programs
- ☐ Unity candles
- ☐ Marriage license
- ☐ Fee for site
- ☐ Fee for officiant
- ☐ Practice bouquet
- ☐ Aisle runner

You might also bring along any last-minute information the wedding party will need, as well as any items that they may be in charge of bringing to the reception.

- ☐ Toasting goblets for reception
- ☐ Cake knife and server

- ☐ Guest book
- ☐ Seating cards for the reception
- ☐ Maps or written directions
- ☐ Wedding day transportation information

The majority of wedding rehearsals are merely a warm-up for the truly important event of the evening: the rehearsal party. The rehearsal party gives everyone involved in the wedding a chance to eat, drink, be merry, and hopefully relax and forget about the stresses of the big day to come.

Traditionally, the expense of the rehearsal party is borne by the groom's parents, but these days anyone who wishes may sponsor the party. A very informal affair, the rehearsal party usually takes place in a restaurant or a private home; a simple phone call is the usual means of inviting the guests.

And who should your host be inviting?

- ☐ All members of the wedding party, along with their spouses or significant others
- ☐ The parents of the bride and groom
- ☐ The ceremony officiant, along with his or her spouse or significant other if this is applicable
- ☐ Any special friends and family members
- ☐ Grandparents of the bride and groom
- ☐ Godparents of the bride and groom
- ☐ Out-of-town wedding guests

Of course, you can invite anyone else you want, but try to keep the party on the intimate side. Remember, the goal of this party is to let everyone relax and give you and your groom some additional time with loved ones who may only be in town for a few days. You'll have plenty of time to party with your other wedding guests on the big day.

A note on children at the rehearsal: Their parents should be invited to the rehearsal party. But unless you are counting on a temper tantrum from an overtired child to be part of the reception entertainment, you should make sure the parents get the children home in time for them to get a good night's sleep.

Rehearsal Party Checklist

RSVP	NAME	PHONE
☐		
☐		
☐		
☐		
☐		
☐		
☐		
☐		
☐		
☐		
☐		
☐		
☐		
☐		
☐		
☐		
☐		
☐		
☐		
☐		
☐		
☐		
☐		
☐		
☐		
☐		
☐		
☐		
☐		
☐		

CHAPTER ELEVEN

What Style!
The Formality
of Your Wedding

*I*n order to properly plan your wedding, it's imperative that you first decide on the type of wedding you want. Though you may be eager to interview musicians, sample caterers' cuisine, view banquet halls, and try on wedding gowns, figuring out your wedding style first will be time well spent and will help guide you through the many decisions you'll have to make later in the game.

The level of your wedding's formality will decide how you rule on everything from the reception site to the attire to how many guests you plan to invite. The following are some general guidelines to follow. Just remember, whatever level of formality you choose, try to keep it more or less consistent throughout.

Very formal:

- Typically held in a church, synagogue, or luxury hotel
- Two hundred or more guests
- Engraved invitations with traditional typeface and wording
- Bride and groom have between four and twelve attendants each
- Bride wears a floor-length gown, cathedral-length train, full-length veil, and long sleeves/arm-covering gloves
- Groom wears cutaway or tails
- Bridesmaids wear matching floor-length dresses or gowns
- Male attendants wear matching cutaway or tails
- Guests don formal attire (white tie for evening)
- Elaborate sit-down dinner, usually held in a ballroom
- Orchestra or live band
- Cascade bouquets and elaborate floral displays
- Limousines or antique cars

Formal:

- Typically held in a church, synagogue, or luxury hotel
- One hundred or more guests
- Engraved or printed invitations with traditional wording
- Bride and groom have between three and six attendants each
- Bride wears a floor-length gown, chapel-length or sweeping train, fingertip veil or hat, and gloves
- Groom wears cutaway or tails
- Bridesmaids wear matching floor-length dresses or gowns
- Male attendants wear matching cutaway or tails
- Guests wear formal attire or evening wear (black tie for evenings)
- Sit-down dinner or buffet, usually held in a ballroom, banquet facility, or private club
- Live band or disc jockey
- Medium-size bouquets and floral displays
- Limousines, antique cars, or horse-drawn carriages

Semiformal:

- Held in a church, synagogue, private home, outdoors, or other location
- Fewer than one hundred guests
- Printed invitations with traditional or personalized wording
- Bride and groom have between one and three attendants each
- Bride wears a floor- or cocktail-length gown with a fingertip veil or hat
- Groom wears a tuxedo, sack coat, or a suit and tie
- Bridesmaids wear matching floor- or cocktail-length dresses

- ॐ Male attendants wear matching tuxes or suits and ties
- ॐ Guests wear evening or business dress
- ॐ Reception including a simple meal or light refreshments usually held at ceremony location, or at a club, garden, restaurant, or home
- ॐ Live band or disc jockey
- ॐ Small bouquet for the bride, simple flower arrangements for decorations

Informal:

- ॐ Daytime ceremony often held at home or in a judge's chambers
- ॐ Fewer than 50 guests
- ॐ Printed or hand-written invitations with personalized wording
- ॐ Bride and groom have one attendant each
- ॐ Bride wears a simple gown, suit, or cocktail-length dress, with no veil or train
- ॐ Groom wears a dark business suit, and tie
- ॐ Maid/matron of honor wears a street-length dress
- ॐ Best man wears a suit and tie
- ॐ Reception including a simple meal or light refreshments, usually held at home, at site of ceremony, or at a restaurant
- ॐ Corsage or small bouquet for the bride, simple flower arrangements for decorations

Reception Sites

The first thing you should do after securing a ceremony date and location is find a reception site. During peak wedding months (April–October) competition for sites is heavy; if you're marrying in this time frame, your best bet is to start looking at least a year in advance.

What are you looking for? You need a site that not only fits into your budget and can hold all your guests, but also presents an appearance and atmosphere you'd be happy with. If you'd like to get away from the traditional banquet hall reception, consider these alternatives:

- Castles, estates, or historic mansions
- Colleges and universities
- Plantations
- Concert halls
- Private or state parks
- Country inns
- Historic villages
- Historic hotels
- Luxury hotels
- Apple orchards
- Beach clubs
- Yachts, ships, boats
- Historic battleships
- Indian reservations or memorial sites
- Theaters
- Aquariums
- Observatories
- Museums
- Galleries
- Public or private gardens
- Nightclubs
- Lighthouses
- Ranches/farmhouses
- Mountain resorts
- Waterfront restaurants
- Greenhouses

Everyone wants a memorable wedding, but some have made the news because they were held in places nobody could forget, such as:

- Underwater
- Hot-air balloon
- Roller coaster
- Bowling alley
- Mountaintop
- Private subway car
- Dirigible
- Skydiving
- Flatbed truck on freeway
- Middle of traffic in rush hour
- Skiing down slope
- Carousel

With any site you decide to visit, make note of architectural details, color schemes, and photography locations. Does the setting suit the mood you want to evoke? How well would this site fit into your dream vision of your wedding?

As easy as it is to get swept up in architecture and atmosphere, there are some practical matters you need to consider. If you find yourself seriously interested in a site, set up an appointment with the site coordinator as soon as possible. Get the following information.

Reception site:_____

Address:_____

_____

_____

Site coordinator:_____

Phone number:_____

Reception site:_____

Address:_____

_____

_____

Site coordinator:_____

Phone number:_____

Reception site:_____

Address:_____

_____

_____

Site coordinator:_____

Phone number:_____

During your meeting, make sure the coordinator can provide satisfactory answers to all of your questions.

- ❏ Is the site conveniently located?
- ❏ What size party can the site accommodate?
- ❏ What rooms are available?
- ❏ For how long is the site available? Is there a time minimum that must be met? Are there overtime charges if the reception runs late?
- ❏ Is there a dance floor? (What size?)
- ❏ Does the site have a catering service? Can you bring in your own caterer if you wish?
- ❏ Does the site provide tables, chairs, dinnerware, linens? What about decorations?
- ❏ Can the facility accommodate live music? Does it have the proper layout, wiring, and equipment?
- ❏ Does the site coordinator have any recommendations for setup and decorations? Can he or she recommend any florists, bands, disc jockeys, and such?

- ☐ Are there any restrictions regarding decorations, music, or photography?
- ☐ Are there any photos of previous receptions that you can see to get the overall feel of the place?
- ☐ What services come with the site? (Waiters, waitresses, bartenders, parking valets?)
- ☐ What is the standard server-to-guest ratio?
- ☐ What kind of reservation deposit is required?
- ☐ Will there be any other weddings at the site on the same day as yours?
- ☐ Is there a package plan? If so, what does it include?
- ☐ Are gratuities included in the price you were quoted?
- ☐ Is there any rental fee for table linens, plants?
- ☐ Does the price vary with the time of day?
- ☐ If it is an outdoor site, what alternate plans are there in case of inclement weather?
- ☐ Will the deposit be returned if you have to cancel?
- ☐ Does the site have a liquor license? Liability insurance?
- ☐ What is the policy on open bars? If you do have an open bar, are you responsible for providing the liquor?
- ☐ Is there a corkage fee? (If you're supplying your own liquor, some sites will charge a corkage fee to cover the costs of the staff opening bottles and pouring drinks.)
- ☐ What are the drink prices at a cash bar?
- ☐ What types of beverages are available?
- ☐ Is there an added price for garnishes for the bar?
- ☐ What is the layout of the tables? How many people does each table seat?

- [ ] Is there enough parking? Is it free? If there is valet parking, what is the policy on rates and gratuities?
- [ ] Is there a coat-check room? Will there be coat-room and restroom attendants? A doorman? What are the charges?
- [ ] Is there a room that can be set aside for picture taking?
- [ ] Are there changing rooms for the bride and groom?
- [ ] Who pays for any police or security that may be required?
- [ ] Can you see references?

Now you should have the facts and figures you need to determine whether or not this site meets your needs and your budget. A deposit (usually a hefty one) will reserve the site you want. But don't hand over any money until you get a written contract stipulating every term of your agreement. Signing a contract will also protect you from becoming a victim of escalating fees, which come into play when a couple reserves a site well in advance of the wedding date. Perhaps you've reserved the site in August for a wedding the following August. If you don't sign a contract specifying this year's prices, the site will try to charge you the new—higher—rates.

Variations on a Theme

While some etiquette aficionados would question the propriety of a theme wedding, there are two schools of thought on this issue. In fact, many believe that taking a step away from convention can make a wedding that much more memorable—both to the couple and to the guests. Depending on the theme you choose, you can live out your fantasies of living in another time or another place—or in a whole new way. Here are some ideas. (Note: Be sure to share whatever theme idea you have with your guests so they can dress appropriately.)

🎐 A period piece: The period wedding theme emphasizes the traditions, costumes, music, and customs of an earlier time period. Though the 1920s through the 1960s are the most popular periods, you could opt for Colonial America or Victorian England if you prefer—as long as you can find the costumes.

🎐 An ethnic flare: There's no better way to say "I'm proud of my heritage" than to orchestrate an ethnic-themed wedding. If you and your fiancé would like to highlight the culture and costumes of your ethnic background, this right here is the theme for you.

🎐 A Western bonanza: Cowboy hats abound at these Western-style weddings. But that's only the tip of the pioneer spirit; also on the menu are fiddles, square dancing, horses, barbecue fare, and anything else that's associated with the wild frontier.

℘ A happy holiday: A wedding set during a holiday season can take advantage of the decorations and spirit of that time. Valentine's Day, with its emphasis on love and romance, is a popular wedding time; Christmas is right up there, too. Easter and Passover are less popular because of certain religious restrictions, but a patriotic motif, complete with fireworks, might be a great idea for the Fourth of July. If you really want to go out on a limb, how about a Halloween wedding, with the wedding party and guests coming in costume and with pumpkins for a centerpiece?

℘ The all-nighter: This is a wedding celebration that's planned to last through the entire night. In some cases, the group rents an additional hall after the first reception. In others, the festivities continue at a private home. The wedding usually comes to a close with breakfast the next morning. Coffee, anyone?

℘ A weekend free-for-all: You've heard of an all-nighter, well this is an all-weekender. Usually, a weekend wedding is set up like a minivacation for you and your guests, and takes place at a resort or hotel.

℘ The honeymoon wedding: Not everyone's cup of tea, but then again not as bad as it sounds. The honeymoon wedding is akin to a weekend wedding. Guests are invited to a romantic honeymoon-type locale such as a resort or an inn, where they can stay with the new couple for a few days. After the honeymoon wedding is over, the bride and groom depart for the real (and much more private) thing.

℘ A moveable feast: Like to travel? In the progressive wedding variation, the bride and groom attend a number of wedding festivities carried on over a period of days—and located in different places! Depending upon your budget, your love of travel, and the availability of friends and relatives to celebrate, you might start with your ceremony on the Eastern Seaboard, have a reception in the Midwest, and wrap things up in California. (Not all progressive wedding celebrations are that far-flung; many stay in the same state, even the same city.)

🪷 "Surprise! You're a Wedding Guest!": The surprise wedding is a surprise not to you (we hope), but to your guests. Invite people to a standard-issue party, and if those in the know can keep a secret, your guests will be completely surprised when they arrive at a wedding.

🪷 A trip down Memory Lane: Stroll down Memory Lane with your groom, family, and friends by having the wedding at a place of special significance to you as a couple. Perhaps you want to return to the college where you two met, or the park where he proposed.

🪷 A no-frills wedding: After all these grand suggestions, it's easy to forget that sometimes the most beautiful and enjoyable weddings are the ones that are the simplest at heart. Without frills and thrills, the meaning of the marriage celebration becomes clearer, and you realize that no matter where you are, it is who you're with that is important.

Meeting, Greeting, and Seating: Reception Decorum

Make sure your wedding isn't something out of a junior high school student's worst nightmare. You know, the one where the poor kid steps on the school bus to find it filled to capacity and not a friendly face in sight. You don't want your guests arriving at a crowded banquet hall and wondering, "Where am I going to sit?"

To ensure that all the invitees have as pleasant a party-going experience as possible, it's important to start off on the right foot with a receiving line and follow through with a well-thought-out seating arrangement. Meanwhile, a head table should go a long way toward making your wedding party happy.

The Receiving Line

The receiving line receives a fair amount of bad press these days, and it's usually the first tradition to get the ax. But while no one is likely to take offense at the omission, a receiving line can be a lot of fun for you and your guests. The tradition enables you, your groom, and key members of the wedding party to meet and greet your guests—which is very important, since you probably will not have time to socialize with everyone at the reception. Imagine painstakingly choosing the perfect gift and traveling for hours to attend a wedding, only to miss out on the opportunity to congratulate the bride and groom. The receiving line is still your best defense against this sad state of affairs.

Traditionally, the receiving line should form after the ceremony but before the reception. You can have it at either site. Just keep in mind that the receiving line is only

as time consuming as you make it. Here's who may participate (in order, beginning at the head of the line):

- 🐚 Bride's mother
- 🐚 Bride's father
- 🐚 Groom's mother
- 🐚 Groom's father
- 🐚 Bride
- 🐚 Groom
- 🐚 Maid of honor (optional)
- 🐚 Best man (optional and not traditional, as the best man is usually left to mingle among the guests)
- 🐚 Bridesmaid (optional)
- 🐚 Usher (optional)
- 🐚 Bridesmaid (optional)
- 🐚 Usher (optional)
- 🐚 Bridesmaid (optional)
- 🐚 Usher (optional)
- 🐚 Bridesmaid (optional)
- 🐚 Usher (optional)
- 🐚 Bridesmaid (optional)
- 🐚 Usher (optional)
- 🐚 Other honor attendant (optional)
- 🐚 Other honor attendant (optional)

The Head Table

The head table is wherever the bride and groom sit, and
is, understandably, the focus of the reception. It usually
faces the other tables, near the dance floor. The table is
sometimes elevated, and decorations or flowers are usually low enough to allow guests a perfect view of you and
your groom.

Traditionally, the bride and groom, honor attendants, bridesmaids, and ushers all sit at the same table. The bride and groom sit in the middle and everyone clusters around as follows:

- Usher
- Bridesmaid
- Usher
- Bridesmaid
- Best man
- Bride
- Groom
- Maid of honor
- Usher
- Bridesmaid
- Usher
- Bridesmaid

While you can always opt to adopt the "rules are made to broken" mentality, tradition dictates that the following people not sit at the head table:

- Parents
- Spouses of attendants
- Children of attendants
- Child attendants

The Seating Plan

Unless you're planning a cocktail reception with hors d'oeuvres or an informal buffet, a seating plan is a must. Guests, especially those who don't know many people, often feel uncomfortable without assigned seating. Though trying to come up with a seating plan that pleases everyone isn't impossible, it may very well seem so at times. Here are the "dos" of putting together a successful seating plan:

🖉 Arrange to sit down with your mother and future mother-in-law to go over the guest list. Make sure that all three of you have equal input on who should sit where and next to whom.

🖉 If you're having a formal wedding, place cards are necessary for all guests.

🖉 At less formal affairs, place cards are only necessary at the head table, while the rest of the guests get table cards. Placed on a table at the reception room entrance, table cards list the name of the guest and their table assignment.

🖉 Another option for less formal weddings is to set up an enlarged seating diagram at the entrance to the reception hall.

🖉 Finally, don't forget that seating your guests can be an opportunity to have fun and show off your creative flair. Here are a few ideas:

• Decorate the tables with centerpieces and other goodies that go along with different themes. For instance, you can outfit every table with a different type of flower.

• Name the tables accordingly. Going with the flower theme, you'll be able to have a Daisy table, a Rose table, and so on.

• When guests arrive, you can tell them where they're sitting by the name of the table.

CHAPTER TWELVE

Picking the
Right Caterer

*I*f your reception site offers an in-house caterer that you find acceptable and that fits your budget, congratulations. Your work is already done! But if you have to find a caterer for yourself, bear in mind that prices and services vary greatly from caterer to caterer. Know what services you want in advance; don't waste your time interviewing candidates that can't provide what you need.

What services do you need? Let's take it from the top.

Time of day of your reception:

- Morning
- Midday
- Midafternoon
- Early evening
- Evening

Style of reception:

- Breakfast/brunch, sit-down dinner
- Breakfast/brunch, buffet
- Brunch/luncheon, sit-down dinner
- Brunch/luncheon, buffet
- Buffet, hors d'oeuvres, cake and coffee
- Cocktail buffet
- Cocktails, dinner, and dance, sit-down
- Cocktails, dinner, and dance, buffet

As you might imagine, the style is largely determined by the time of day you select.

Here are a few basic guidelines:

Luncheon wedding: Between 12:00 and 2:00
Tea reception: Between 2:00 and 4:00
Cocktail reception: Between 4:00 and 7:30
Dinner reception: Between 7:00 and 9:00

Caterer Choices

All caterers are not created equal. When shopping around, you'll no doubt be confronted with a variety of options. Here's the skinny on every caterer under the sun.

In-House Caterers

These are made available by your reception site, and are usually located on the premises.

Credits:

- Offered by all hotels and most country clubs
- Saves you the trouble of finding a caterer yourself
- In-house caterers are already familiar with the particulars of the room, and can offer a lot of suggestions

Debits:

- Usually more expensive than independent catering
- May offer all-inclusive packages that prohibit you from entering into any agreements with subcontractors

Independent Caterers

Independent caterers come in all shapes and sizes. Each offers a different degree of service so there's no reason to settle for anything less than sheer perfection. The following are some of the main types that you're likely to encounter.

Bare Bones Caterers

Some caterers specialize in keeping it simple—they provide food and food only. Everything else, and we mean everything, has to come from you and you alone.

Credits:
- Enable you to save money on various services
- Often offer good food at a low price
- Allow you to buy alcohol in bulk and avoid the outrageous markups that usually accompany an open bar

Debits:
- Don't provide linens
- Don't provide dinnerware
- Don't provide glasses
- Don't provide a waitstaff
- Inconvenience you, the busy bride and groom, by forcing you to work out all the details on your own

Some-Meat-on-Their-Bones Caterers

This is the most popular type of caterer and the type that most people associate with a wedding reception.

Credits:
- Provide food
- Provide beverages
- Provide a waitstaff
- Provide bartenders
- Most provide linens and dinnerware
- Usually agree to provide tables and chairs, for a fee

Debits:
- Most will not allow you to provide your own alcohol
- May tack on exorbitant fees for equipping you with necessities such as tables and chairs

Fat Cat(erer)s

As you would expect, this type of caterer offers just about every item and service you could possibly imagine, as well as a few you probably couldn't. Many of these caterers have branched out into the reception coordinating business. Basically, if you choose to pay them for it, you can spend the months before your wedding in worry-free bliss, and leave the reception planning to the caterer.

Credits:
- Will take care of everything: the flowers, the music, the photographer, the whole nine yards

Debits:
- High price tag—this kind of service redefines the term "expensive"
- Leaves you powerless to choose your own service providers
- With so much to be done, quality may get lost in the planning process

There are some questions to ask potential caterers:

☐ What is the caterer's background and experience? (How many weddings has the firm handled? What was the largest? The smallest? Are references available?)

☐ Are package deals available? (In other words, can the caterer supply elements of the standard ser-

vice—flowers and meals, say—and leave other elements—such as liquor—in your hands?)

❑ Is there an added charge for the staff's
working time?

❑ Will you need to rent or borrow any serving
pieces? (i.e., tables, chairs, equipment)

❑ Is the caterer in the restaurant business?
(This is usually a good sign.)

❑ What color linens can the caterer supply, if any?

❑ What kind of glassware does the caterer supply
(wine/champagne stemware), if any?

❑ Are china and silverware part of the package?

❑ Can they supply the cake?

❑ Will the caterer try to charge you a "cake-cutting
fee"? (If so, negotiate your way out of this, or find
someone else. This charge is nothing but an
excuse to pay people twice. Don't agree to do it.)

❑ Can you taste test the meal options. (You might
also want to ask to observe another wedding the
firm is catering.)

❑ Are taxes and gratuities included in the package?

❑ When do you have to supply the final guest count?

❑ If necessary, can the caterer provide bartenders?

❑ Can the firm supply valet services if needed?

❑ Is there a list of client references you can contact?

❑ How will the fee be structured. Is it a flat rate, an
hourly rate, or a package deal?

❑ How much of a deposit is required?

Finally, ask the Better Business Bureau to supply you with information about any complaints that may have been filed against the firm. When working with a private caterer, make sure that all services and financial agreements are clearly understood.

Once you decide on a caterer, you will want to work together to establish your menu.

- ℘ Will the meal be served buffet-style? Sit-down-style? Russian-style (guests served food from platters brought to their tables)?
- ℘ What hors d'oeuvres will be served (if any)?
- ℘ What main course(s) will be served?
- ℘ What dessert(s) will be served?

If your reception site does not provide bar service, you are responsible for stocking the bar. Important note! If you will be operating the bar yourself, it must be an open bar (unless you have a liquor license). Selling liquor without a license is illegal.

Alcoholic Beverages

The following should be available at the bar.

- ☐ Beer
- ☐ Wine
- ☐ Hard liquor
- ☐ Champagne
- ☐ Mixers
- ☐ Lemons, limes, cherries, olives
- ☐ Soda and other nonalcoholic beverages
- ☐ Champagne punch
- ☐ Nonalcoholic punch

Extras

Aside from the menu, what additional services will the caterer be providing? Ask about . . .

- ☐ Waiters/waitresses
- ☐ Bartenders
- ☐ Valets

What equipment, if any, will you need to get from the caterer or rent yourself? Find out about . . .

- ☐ Tables and chairs
- ☐ Linens
- ☐ Dinnerware, glassware, silverware
- ☐ Coffee service

Caterer Checklist

Item	Description	Cost
☐ Appetizers		
☐ Entrees		
☐ Dessert		
☐ Other food		
☐ Beverages		
☐ Nonalcoholic		
☐ Champagne		
☐ Wine		
☐ Liquor		
☐ Equipment		
☐ Tent		
☐ Chairs		
☐ Tables		
☐ Linens		
☐ Dinnerware		
☐ Flatware		
☐ Glassware		
☐ Serving pieces		
☐ Other		
☐ Service		
☐ Servers		
☐ Bartenders		
☐ Valet parking		
☐ Attendants		
☐ Coat checkers		
☐ Overtime cost		

It's a Deal!

Once everything's been decided on . . .

- ☐ Get every part of the agreement in writing (costs, services, date, time). The caterer should provide you with an estimated cost per person.
- ☐ Make sure the caterer is (or will be) well acquainted with the reception site and its facilities.
- ☐ Work up the final guest count and give it to the caterer.
- ☐ Ask the caterer whether the final cost per guest will differ from the initial estimate. If it will, ask by how much.

Caterer Information

Name (if different from reception site): _____

_____

Address: _____

_____

Telephone: _____

Contact: _____

CHAPTER THIRTEEN

Photography and Videography: Nothing but the Best

*Y*ou're spending a bundle on this wedding. Why not have some decent pictures to remember the day by? Of all the people and places you'll shell out money to over the course of your wedding, your photographer will be one of the most important. Imagine how heartbroken you'd be to find that the supposedly professional photographer you hired could only produce blurry, muddy photos—or worse yet, took all the photos with the lens cap on!

It may sound absurd, but such nightmares are not at all uncommon. Don't let yourself become another victim. Choose your photographer carefully; only sign on with someone after you've seen his or her work and checked references.

Here is a list of questions that will help you choose the best man, woman, or studio for the job.

- [ ] How long has the photographer been in this business?
- [ ] Does the photographer specialize in weddings? (If he or she isn't a wedding expert, find someone who is.)
- [ ] Is this a full-time photographer? (Part-timers need not apply.)
- [ ] Can you see samples of previous work and speak to some former clients?
- [ ] What types of photo packages are offered?
- [ ] What is included in the standard package?
- [ ] What are the costs for additional photos?
- [ ] How many pictures does the photographer typically take at a wedding of this size?
- [ ] In addition to the base package fee, will there be any additional hourly fees? Travel costs?
- [ ] Will you be charged by the hour?

- ❏ Does the photographer keep negatives? If so, for how long?
- ❏ May you purchase negatives if you wish?
- ❏ Will you be able to purchase extra photos in the future?
- ❏ Does the photographer use a variety of lighting techniques? A variety of backgrounds?
- ❏ Will the photographer take a mixture of formal and candid shots?
- ❏ Would the photographer be willing to incorporate your ideas into the shot list?
- ❏ Will the photographer provide a contract stipulating services, date, time, costs, and so on?

It's always wise to interview more than one photographer. That way, you can compare quality and prices to get the best person (and the best deal) for you.

Click, Click, Click Goes the Shutter

Once you decide on a photographer, sit down with him or her to talk about the type and amount of photographs you'd like to see come out of your wedding. Remember, your photographer is there to meet your needs, but he or she won't be able to incorporate your ideas unless you communicate them.

The Hit List

Make up a list of the posed pictures you'll want the photographer to take on your wedding day. Here are some suggestions.

- [ ] You and your groom
- [ ] You alone with your mother
- [ ] You alone with your father
- [ ] You with your mother and father
- [ ] You with the groom's parents
- [ ] The groom alone with his mother
- [ ] The groom alone with his father
- [ ] The groom with his mother and father
- [ ] The groom with your parents
- [ ] You and the groom with both sets of parents
- [ ] You with your attendants in a group
- [ ] The groom with his attendants in a group
- [ ] The whole wedding party
- [ ] You and the groom with grandparents, godparents, and/or any favorite relatives

The Bridal Portrait

Before sitting down for your solo shot, make sure you have:

- ℘ Your gown
- ℘ A hat, veil, or other headpiece you select
- ℘ Gloves, if you plan to wear them
- ℘ Wedding shoes and stockings
- ℘ Jewelry you plan to wear on your wedding day
- ℘ A bridal bouquet (if you can't get one from your florist, the bridal salon or studio can usually provide models)

You're on Candid Camera!

You'll also want candid shots of the ceremony and reception.

Candid shots before the ceremony:

- ☐ You and your attendants at your home before the ceremony
- ☐ Informal shots of you and your attendants at the back of the church or ceremony site
- ☐ Informal shots of you and your father before the ceremony
- ☐ You and your father arriving at the ceremony getting out of the car, and walking into the ceremony site
- ☐ You and your groom getting into the car
- ☐ You and the groom toasting one another in the car

Traditional ceremony "candids":

- ☐ Each attendant walking down the aisle, including flower girls, ringbearer, and pages
- ☐ Your mother coming down the aisle
- ☐ The groom's parents coming down the aisle

- ☐ You and your father coming down the aisle
- ☐ Your father leaving you at the altar
- ☐ Wedding party at the altar
- ☐ You and the groom exchanging vows and rings
- ☐ The lighting of candles and any other special ceremony features
- ☐ You and the groom kissing at the altar
- ☐ You and the groom leaving the ceremony

Reception candids:

- ☐ You and your groom arriving at the reception
- ☐ Your first dance with the groom
- ☐ You dancing with your father
- ☐ The groom dancing with his mother
- ☐ Cutting the cake and feeding it to each other
- ☐ Toasting each other
- ☐ Tossing the garter
- ☐ Tossing the bouquet
- ☐ You and the groom leaving the reception
- ☐ The "getaway" car
- ☐ Any other candid shots

Front-Page News?

If you're planning to send a wedding announcement to the newspaper, be sure to inform your photographer so he or she can take a black-and-white portrait of the two of you as man and wife. Order a 5" × 7" glossy print to send to the paper.

Taping Your Wedding

With VCRs a standard feature in most American homes, it should come as no surprise that wedding videotapes are now as popular as traditional still photographs. How else are the bride and groom going to see and hear everything they were too excited or dazed to be aware of while it was actually happening?

Most couples consider their wedding videotape priceless, but that doesn't mean you have to shell out the family fortune to get a good one. As with still photography, you should be very careful about who you choose to trust with the valuable responsibility of videotaping your wedding. Ask the same types of questions and apply the same scrutiny that you did when choosing a photographer.

Here are some things you'll want to ask your videographer.

- ☐ How long has the person been doing this professionally?
- ☐ Can you see samples of the work and check references?
- ☐ Is the work guaranteed?
- ☐ Can you look at a work in progress in addition to a demo tape? (This way you'll know that the videographer is actually doing the work, not buying great demo tapes from someone else.)
- ☐ Is the equipment high-quality, including the editing and dubbing machines?
- ☐ Will the videographer be using a high-quality tape?
- ☐ How many cameras will be used? How big will the videographer's staff be?
- ☐ What special effects are available?
- ☐ Will you use wireless microphones during the ceremony so that the vows will be clearly heard on the tape?

☐ How is the fee computed? One flat rate?
   By the hour?
☐ Is a standard package deal offered?
   If so, what is it?
☐ Are there ways to cut down on the total price?
☐ How much will it cost to have copies of the original made?

When viewing sample tapes, consider the following questions.

☐ Do the segments tell a story, giving a clear sense of the order in which the events took place?
☐ Does the tape capture the most important moments—such as you cutting the cake and throwing the garter?
☐ Is there steady use of the camera, clear sound, vibrant color, and a nice sharp picture?
☐ How are the shots framed? What editing techniques are used?
☐ Does the tape move smoothly from one scene to the next—rather than lurching ahead unexpectedly?

Watch Out!

It's usually not a wise idea to hire a family member or friend to be your videographer, even if they do have a shiny new camera. They may do adequate work, but odds are they still can't provide you with the same quality you'll get from a professional. (They probably won't have the necessary editing equipment, for one thing.) Friends and relatives are also more likely to get caught up in the action and forget that they're supposed to be filming it!

With all of the equipment and technology available today, you should settle for nothing less than a broadcast-quality wedding video. Get the best deal for your money, but don't choose someone cheap and incompetent over someone who'll cost a little more but do a wonderful job.

Obviously, you'll want to interview more than one videographer.

Finally, when you are sure you've found the videographer you want, ask to sign a contract with details such as date, location, starting time, number of cameras, amount of editing, name of camera person, names of any assistants, end time, and most important, the final cost.

Putting Everything in Place

Once you select a videographer, take some time to discuss the type of video you want. You will need to . . .

- ❏ Find out whether your ceremony site puts any restrictions on camera placement.
- ❏ Take your videographer to the ceremony site so he or she can see the working conditions.
- ❏ Arrange for your videographer and photographer to meet (if they don't already know each other) so that they can get acquainted and coordinate their activities.

Name That Format

There are various format options for wedding videos. Here are a few you might like to consider.

The Nostalgic Format

This type of video usually starts with vintage photographs of you and your groom, perhaps as children or young adults. From there, it can show the two of you sharing your lives together. The ceremony, reception, and (sometimes) shots of your honeymoon end this format. Because it takes a little more work to put together, this type of video can be expensive.

The Straight Shot Format

This format uses only one camera, thus making it the least expensive video option offered. No editing is required, but the videographer can still add small touches, such as names and dates, to help spice up the film.

The Documentary Format

As its title suggests, this format gives you a documentary style account of your wedding day. It usually starts with you and your groom getting ready, then proceeds to scenes of the ceremony and the reception; sometimes interviews with family and friends are added. The documentary format has become quite popular; the price will vary widely depending on the type of equipment used and the amount of editing needed.

The Last Word on Video

Be sure to ask your videographer about any new technological advances in cameras, tapes, or editing that you might be able to take advantage of. Because technology develops so fast, there may be equipment available now that was unheard of last year. Currently, advances are being made with the new eight millimeter tape format. The eight millimeter tape provides a very high quality image and stands the test of time better than the standard VHS tape.

Photographer Worksheet

Name of photographer/studio:

Address:

Telephone:

Contact:

Hours they can be reached:

Directions:

Appointments:

Date: Time:

Date: Time:

Date: Time:

Name of package (if applicable):

Date of hired services: Time:

Number of hours:

Overtime cost:

Travel fee:

Fee for custom pages:

Fee for black and white prints:

Fee for sepia prints:

Fee for album inscription:

Additional fees (if any):

Engagement session included? _Yes   _No

Additional cost (if any):

Will attend rehearsal? _Yes   _No

Additional cost (if any):

Cost of film, proofing, and processional included? _Yes _No

Additional cost, if any:

Type of wedding album included:

Date proofs will be ready: Date order will be ready:

Additional services included:

Cost: Total amount due:

Amount of deposit: Date:

Balance due: Date:

Sales tax included? _Yes   _No

Terms of cancellation:

Notes:

Included in Package:

Number: Cost of Each

Notes:

Item:

Included:

Additional:

8" x 10" engagement portraits:

5" x 7" engagement prints:

4" x 5" engagement prints:

Wallet-size engagement prints:

Wedding proofs:

Wallet-size prints:

3" x 5" prints:

4" x 5" prints:

5" x 7" prints:

11" x 14" portraits:

Other prints (list below):

Preview album:

Wedding album:

Wedding album pages:

Parent albums:

Other (list below):

Videographer Worksheet

Name of videographer/studio:

Address:

Telephone: Contact:

Hours they can be reached:

Directions:

Appointments:

Date: Time:

Date: Time:

Date: Time:

Name of package (if applicable):

Date of hired services: Time:

Number of hours: Number of cameras:

Overtime cost: Travel fee:

Additional fees (if any):

Will attend rehearsal? _Yes   _No

Additional cost, if any:

Length of videotape:

Date tape will be ready:

Videotape will include:

Prewedding preparations? _Yes _No

Notes:

Individual interviews with bride and groom prior to ceremony? _Yes _No

Notes:

Ceremony?   _Yes   _No

Notes:

Reception?   _Yes   _No

Notes:

Photo montage?   _Yes   _No

Notes:

Other:

Package includes:

Sound? _Yes _No

Notes:

Music? _Yes _No

Notes:

Unedited version of wedding events? _Yes _No

Notes:

Edited version of wedding events? _Yes _No

Notes:

Price of additional copies of videotape:

Other:

Additional services included: Cost:

Total amount due:

Amount of deposit: Date:

Balance due: Date:

Sales tax included? _Yes _No

Terms of cancellation:

Notes:

CHAPTER FOURTEEN

Reception
Music

As soon as you've set a date for your wedding, you'll want to start thinking about hiring entertainment for your reception. Most reception entertainment consists of a live band or a DJ, either of which should be reserved about three to six months in advance of your wedding date. Ask for suggestions from family and friends; if they come up empty, hit some area clubs and lounges and start listening. Before long, you'll understand why the good bands and DJs are always booked. You may have to dig a little to find someone you're happy with, but in the end, finding the right music option for you and your guests can make all the effort worthwhile.

What to look (and listen) for in a band:

- Do you like the group's sound?
  (Is it appropriate for your wedding?)
- How good is the band's sound system?
- Is their overall appearance and demeanor positive?
  (Do band members look happy about what they're doing?)
- Do they have a wide repertoire of material?
  (Do they balance various styles well? Is there a good mix of fast and slow songs?)
- Would you trust the band leader to serve as master of ceremonies if need be?
  (Will he or she charge extra for this?)

You may decide that the best music option for your reception is a disk jockey. Hiring a DJ has several advantages: the selection of songs is greater, the logistical hassles are fewer, and the cost is less than a band's. However, many people consider a disk jockey to be a sign of a somewhat informal reception.

What to look (and listen) for in a DJ:

- ✍ Is the equipment and sound system of good quality?
- ✍ Does the DJ have a large selection of records you and your guests will like?
- ✍ Does he or she mix different sounds and styles well? Is there a good mix of fast and slow songs?
- ✍ Would you trust him or her to serve as master of ceremonies, if need be? (Is there any additional fee for this?)

Once you find someone you like, it's time to talk terms:

- ✍ What are the costs?
- ✍ Are there any added fees not included in the quote?
- ✍ Will the DJ's/band's attire be appropriate for the reception?
- ✍ Is a special sound system or hookup required?
- ✍ What is the cancellation policy?
- ✍ What are the payment terms?
  (Ask about deposit and balance amounts.)
- ✍ What are the hourly overtime rates?
- ✍ If songs that are important to you are not currently in the repertoire or play list, can they be added? Is there any additional charge for this?

And before you sign on the dotted line try to get the answers to these questions too. (You may want to visit the site with your band or DJ before making any formal commitment.)

- ☐ Can the reception site accommodate your band or DJ?
- ☐ Is there enough electrical power? Outlets? Space?
- ☐ How are the acoustics?

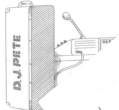

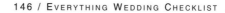

Get It in Writing

Some details should never be left to chance, so make sure to get the following stipulations in writing.

☐ The attire. You don't want to see anyone wearing ripped jeans and gym shorts to a formal wedding, much less to *your* formal wedding.

☐ The arrival time. Make sure that the band or DJ has enough lead time to set up their gear before the guests arrive. This is especially important for bands, as sound checks don't often make for soothing dinner music.

☐ The exact cost of the services, and everything that price includes. Some bands charge you if they have to add an extra piece of equipment; some DJs charge for extra trips to the record store. Find out in advance about everything you'll be expected to pay for.

☐ The band's or DJ's knowledge of the exact location of the reception. Sounds elementary? Well, believe it or not, there have actually been instances where the musical talent has shown up at the right hotel, but in the wrong city!

List of Requests

Bride and groom's first dance:_____

Bride and her father: _____

Groom and his mother: _____

Bride and groom's parents: _____

Cake cutting: _____

Bride tossing the bouquet: _____

Groom throwing the garter: _____

Bride and groom leaving the reception: _____

Additional requests:

_____

_____

_____

Name of band/DJ:

Address:

Telephone:

Manager/contact:

Hours he or she can be reached:

Number of performers:

Description of act:

Demo tape available? _Yes   _No

Notes:

View live performances?   _Yes   _No

Date: Time: Location:

Appointments:

Date: Time:

Date: Time:

Date: Time:

Date of hired services: Time:

Number of hours:

Cocktail hour:

Overtime cost: Includes the following services:

Equipment provided:

Equipment rented:

Rental costs: Cost:

Total amount due: Amount of deposit:

Date: Balance due:

Date: Terms of cancellation:

Notes:

Tearjerkers

If you're stuck for ideas, consider some of these reception favorites (and the people who made them famous):

- ☐ "Sunrise, Sunset," from *Fiddler on the Roof*
- ☐ "Daddy's Little Girl," Burke and Gerlach
- ☐ "You Are the Sunshine of My Life," Stevie Wonder
- ☐ "Just the Way You Are," Billy Joel
- ☐ "On the Wings of Love," Jeffrey Osborne
- ☐ "Here and Now," Luther Vandross
- ☐ "Truly," Lionel Ritchie
- ☐ "Hopelessly Devoted to You," Olivia Newton-John
- ☐ "Endless Love," Diana Ross and Lionel Ritchie
- ☐ "Up Where We Belong," Joe Cocker and Jennifer Warnes
- ☐ "Waiting for a Girl Like You," Foreigner
- ☐ "The Wind Beneath My Wings," Bette Midler
- ☐ "Pretty Woman," Roy Orbison
- ☐ "Just Because," Anita Baker
- ☐ "I Won't Last a Day Without You," Andy Williams
- ☐ "Through the Eyes of Love," Sager and Hamlisch
- ☐ "In Your Eyes," Peter Gabriel
- ☐ "The Glory of Love," Peter Cetera
- ☐ "Always," Starpoint
- ☐ "Could I Have This Dance?" Anne Murray

- ☐ "Lady Love," Lou Rawls
- ☐ "Just the Two of Us," Grover Washington
- ☐ "Inspiration," Chicago
- ☐ "Time in a Bottle," Jim Croce
- ☐ "Unforgettable," Nat King Cole (or with Natalie Cole)
- ☐ "Unchained Melody," Righteous Brothers
- ☐ "Here, There, and Everywhere," The Beatles
- ☐ "September Morn," Neil Diamond
- ☐ "Silly Love Songs," Paul McCartney
- ☐ "The Wedding Song," Paul Stookey
- ☐ "As Time Goes By," from *Casablanca*
- ☐ "Woman," John Lennon
- ☐ "Ribbon in the Sky," Stevie Wonder
- ☐ "Wonderful Tonight," Eric Clapton
- ☐ "We've Only Just Begun," The Carpenters
- ☐ "Misty," Johnny Mathis
- ☐ "I Love You So," Andy Williams
- ☐ "Beginnings," Chicago
- ☐ "I Do (Cherish You)" 98 Degrees
- ☐ "Theme from Ice Castles," Melissa Manchester

If you're like most couples, you will have special songs in mind that you want played at key points of the reception. List them here and you'll have a written record to share with your DJ or master of ceremonies.

Introduce entire bridal party? ❏ Yes ❏ No
Music: _____
Introduce only bride and groom? ❏ Yes ❏ No
Music: _____
Parent(s) of bride: _____
Parent(s) of groom: _____
Grandparent(s) of bride: _____
Grandparent(s) of groom: _____
Flower girl(s): _____
Ring bearer(s): _____
Bridesmaids: _____
_____
Ushers: _____
_____
Maid of honor: _____
Best man: _____
Matron of honor:_____
Bride's first name: _____
Groom's first name: _____
Bride and groom as they are to be introduced:
_____
Receiving line at reception? ❏ Yes ❏ No   When: _____
Music: _____
Blessing? ❏ Yes ❏ No
By whom: _____
First toast? ❏ Yes ❏ No
By whom: _____

Other toasts? ❑ Yes ❑ No

By whom: _____

_____

First dance: ❑ Yes ❑ No

Music: _____

To join in first dance:

Maid of honor and best man? ❑ Yes ❑ No

Parents of bride and groom? ❑ Yes ❑ No

Bridesmaids and ushers? ❑ Yes ❑ No

Guests? ❑ Yes ❑ No

Father-daughter dance? ❑ Yes ❑ No

Music: _____

Mother-son dance? ❑ Yes ❑ No

Music: _____

Open dance floor for guests after first dance? ❑ Yes ❑ No

Cake-cutting? ❑ Yes ❑ No

Music: _____

Bouquet toss? ❑ Yes ❑ No

Garter toss? ❑ Yes ❑ No

Last dance? ❑ Yes ❑ No

Music: _____

Other event: _____

When: _____

Music: _____

CHAPTER FIFTEEN

Flower Power: Your Wedding Flowers

With all this hectic wedding rush, wouldn't you like to sit back and take some time to smell the roses? Well, wait until you find a florist and choose your flower arrangements. Otherwise, there won't be any roses to smell!

Try to find a florist who comes with good recommendations from family or friends. Once you've selected a florist, make an appointment to meet with him or her to discuss your overall needs. (Be sure you have sample fabric of all the attendants' dresses on hand so you can match colors if you need to.)

Before you pick your wedding flowers, take a look at this list of their various meanings.

- Amaryllis: splendid beauty
- Apple blossoms: temptation
- Bachelor's button: celibacy or hope (depending on who you talk to)
- Bluebell: constancy
- Buttercup: riches
- Camellia: perfect loveliness, gratitude
- Carnation: pure, deep love
- Daffodil: regard
- Daisy: share your feelings
- Forget-me-not: don't forget (or true love)
- Gardenia: joy
- Honeysuckle: generous and devoted affection, genuine affection
- Ivy: fidelity
- Jasmine: amiability, (or grace and elegance)
- Jonquil: affection returned
- Lily: purity
- Lily of the valley: happiness

- 🌿 Lime: conjugal bliss
- 🌿 Marigold: sacred affection
- 🌿 Myrtle: love
- 🌿 Orange blossom: purity, loveliness
- 🌿 Red chrysanthemum: I love you
- 🌿 Red rose: I love you
- 🌿 Red tulip: love declared
- 🌿 Rose: love
- 🌿 Violet: modesty (or faithfulness)
- 🌿 White camellia: perfect loveliness
- 🌿 White daisy: innocence
- 🌿 White lilac: first emotions of love
- 🌿 White lily: purity and innocence
- 🌿 Wood sorrel: joy

Who and what will you be needing flowers for? This list below should give you a good idea.

Flowers for the Women
The bride:

- ☐ Bridal bouquet

Optional:

- ☐ A smaller bouquet, to throw at the bouquet toss
- ☐ Floral headdress
- ☐ Going-away corsage

To be delivered to: _____

Time: _____ Cost: _____

Bridal attendants:

- ☐ Matron of honor
- ☐ Maid of honor
- ☐ Bridesmaids
- ☐ Flower girl
- ☐ Floral headdresses (if desired)

To be delivered to: _____

Time: _____ Cost: _____

Flowers for the Men
The Groom and his attendants:

- ☐ Groom's boutonniere
- ☐ Best man's boutonniere
- ☐ Ushers' boutonniere
- ☐ Ringbearer's boutonniere

To be delivered to: _____
Time: _____ Cost: _____

Flowers for the Family and Special Friends

- ☐ Bride's mother
- ☐ Groom's mother
  - Optional:
- ☐ Stepmother
- ☐ Grandmothers
- ☐ Mothers' roses
- ☐ Aunts, cousins, special friends

To be delivered to: _____
Time: _____ Cost: _____

Flowers for Wedding Helpers and Participants

- ☐ Bridal consultant
- ☐ Officiant
- ☐ Soloist
- ☐ Readers
- ☐ Instrumentalist
- ☐ Guest book attendant
- ☐ Gift attendant
- ☐ Others

To be delivered to: _____
Time: _____ Cost: _____

Now that you've taken care of the people, it's time to start thinking about flowers for all of your wedding places.

Ceremony Site
- ☐ Arch/Canopy
- ☐ Candelabra
- ☐ Altar floral spray
- ☐ Pews
- ☐ Aisles (runner)
- ☐ Other
- ☐ Kneeling cushion (for bride and groom)

To be delivered to: _____
Time: _____ Cost: _____

Rehearsal Dinner Site
- ☐ Centerpieces

To be delivered to: _____
Time: _____ Cost: _____

Reception Site
- ☐ Decorations, centerpieces for tables
- ☐ Main table
- ☐ Cake table
- ☐ Gift table
- ☐ Drapes, garland, or greenery
- ☐ Flower petals for tossing
- ☐ Powder room
- ☐ Top of cake (if desired)
- ☐ Hanging plants
- ☐ Small trees
- ☐ Deposit left

To be delivered to: _____
Time: _____ Cost: _____

If you use a lot of floral arrangements at your wedding, put someone in charge of dispensing them after the reception. You may want to give the flowers to close friends or relatives, or perhaps to nursing homes or charitable organizations.

Record of Florist

Florist name: _____

Phone: _____

Address: _____

_____

Dates orders were placed: _____

Questions for Your Florist

- ☐ Do you have arrangements that will fit my budget?
- ☐ Do you have photos of previous displays you've done?
- ☐ Can I have a list of references?
- ☐ Can you match or complement the color scheme of my wedding? (bring color swatches)
- ☐ Will you be able to come to the ceremony reception sites to get a feel for what kinds of flower arrangements are needed?
- ☐ Can you arrive before the photographer so that everything is ready by picture time?
- ☐ Can you provide me with a written contract stipulating all costs, times, dates, places, and services?

A Bouquet for Posterity

Many brides choose to preserve their bridal bouquet as a memento of the wedding. In reality, the odds are very strong that your bouquet will end up in storage (which is

often just a fancy way of saying "someplace no one remembers"). Keep this in mind if you decide to take your bouquet to the florist for preservation; the process will probably cost you more than the bouquet itself. There are, however, cheaper and more practical ways for you to preserve your bouquet yourself. Here are guidelines for a few of the most popular.

Pressing

This is the single most popular means of bouquet preservation. The steps to successfully pressing your bouquet are as follows. (Note: The process works best when it's started soon after the wedding, because the flowers have had less time to wilt. If you ask real nice and promise to return the favor, you might just be able to convince your maid of honor to do it while you're on your honeymoon.)

- Take a picture of your bouquet; you'll need it to refer to later.
- Take the bouquet apart (and that's no typo).
- Place the separate flowers in the pages of heavy books, between sheets of blank white paper. (Warning: if you neglect to cushion with blank paper, ink from the book's pages will ruin the flowers.)
- Keep flowers in books for two to six weeks, depending on their size. (Hint: the bigger the flower, the more time it will need.)
- When the flowers look ready, glue them onto a mounting board in an arrangement that closely resembles the original bouquet in the photo.
- Place the board in a picture frame.
- Hang wherever your heart desires.

Hanging/Drying

As with pressing, the earlier you start the process, the more successful it's likely to be. Here are the steps:

- Snap a photo for future reference.
- Take the bouquet apart.
- Hang the flowers upside down to dry, thereby preventing drooping and keeping the flowers' shape in tact (some color may be lost in the drying process, but this can be averted if the flowers are hung in a dark room).
- When the flowers are completely dry, spray them with shellac or silica gel for protection.
- Reassemble flowers to match the photo.

Potpourri

This is a novel take on preserving the bridal bouquet, as it involves tearing the whole thing apart. In the end, however, you'll never have to be without a little piece of your wedding.

- Buy some netting or lacy fabric.
- Buy some thin ribbon.
- Cut the netting into four-inch squares.
- Dry the flowers.
- Gather the petals together.
- Place small piles of the petals into the four-inch squares of netting.
- Tie the squares into little pouches with the ribbon.
- Place these little sachets anywhere you wish to fill the air with a small reminder of your wedding day.

CHAPTER SIXTEEN

The Cake

*L*ong ago in medieval England, it was customary for each guest to bring a small cake or bun to a wedding. These days, the marrying couple is responsible for providing their own cake. The wedding cakes of today are no simple affair; they may require a small army of bakers (and large chunks of time and money) to put together. Unless you can convince your guests they're in medieval England, here's what you're going to have to do:

- ☐ Begin searching for a bakery at least three months before the wedding.
- ☐ View the bakeries' sample books to find the right cake for you.
- ☐ Ask for taste tests of any style cake you're seriously considering.
- ☐ If the wedding cake is going to serve as dessert, tell the baker how many guests you expect.
- ☐ Find out how much of a deposit is required.
- ☐ Find out if the deposit is refundable.
- ☐ Ask about any additional delivery or rental charges.
- ☐ Ask whether there will be a fee for having the baker set up the cake at the reception site.
- ☐ Ask whether the baker will supply a cake knife. (If not, you'll have to buy one.)
- ☐ If you want someone from the bakery to stay at the reception to help cut and serve the cake, find out the cost for this service.
- ☐ Arrange when final payment for the cake is due.
- ☐ Order the cake.
- ☐ Get a written contract stipulating type of cake, cost, date of delivery, and any other important specifications.

☐ Arrange for the baker to arrive at the reception
site before the guests to set up the cake.
☐ Decide where the cake will be displayed: on the
head table or on a table of its own.

A Matter of Taste ... and Design

Gone are the days of the plain white wedding cake with
plain white frosting. The choices for cake flavors, frostings,
decorations, and garnishing are plentiful—and tempting.
Here are just a few.

Cake flavors:

- Chocolate
- Double chocolate
- Vanilla
- White
- Spice
- Carrot cake
- Cheese cake
- Citron chiffon
- Fruitcake
- Chocolate hazelnut
- Italian rum
- Lemon
- Orange
- Raspberry
- Strawberry
- Chocolate mousse
- Chocolate mocha spice
- Banana

Fillings:

- Lemon
- Raspberry
- Coffee
- Strawberry
- Vanilla
- Butter cream
- Custard

Sauces/toppings:

- Ice cream
- Fresh fruit
- Sweet fruit sauce
- Hot chocolate sauce

And that's just the flavors! Your cake can be designed any number of ways, too—including multiple tiers, stacked cakes, multiple sections, and even fountains! With so many options, coming to a final decision can be pretty hard. Here's a list of questions to ask your baker that might narrow things down a bit.

- ☐ What size cake should you have for the number of guests you're having?
- ☐ Can you have different flavors for different layers of the cake?
- ☐ What choices are available in cake flavors and frostings?
- ☐ Does the baker specialize in any flavor, style, or size?
- ☐ Is there a rental fee for tiers or separators?
- ☐ Can a small portion of the cake be prepared with brandy or another form of alcohol? (This will make it easier to eat a year from now if you decide to follow the tradition of freezing a small quantity of cake and sharing it with your husband on your first anniversary.)
- ☐ Is a cake knife provided, or do you have to buy your own?

Some weddings also feature a groom's cake, traditionally a dark fruit-cake packed into white boxes and given to the guests as a gift. Not everyone has a groom's cake these days. Couples who do often take a lighthearted approach and have the cake decorated to resemble a hobby of the groom's. If your

groom is a baseball fan, you might decide to have the cake shaped like a bat or a ball.

Usually, the same baker makes both the wedding cake and the groom's cake.

- ☐ Pick a cake flavor and design. (It doesn't have to be fruitcake any more!)
- ☐ Order the cake.
- ☐ Arrange for payment, delivery, and so on. Try to get a written contract just as you would with a wedding cake.

Bakery name: _____

Address: _____

Phone: _____

Contact: _____

Cake flavors: _____ Cost: _____

_____ Cost: _____

_____ Cost: _____

Icing (frosting): _____

Number of tiers: _____

Ornaments: _____

Samples: _____

_____

Notes: _____

_____

_____

DIY Cake Service

Now you can cut your cake and eat it too! In case neither the baker nor the caterer is there to help you out, here's a quick guide to serving your own wedding cake.

1. Cut vertically through the bottom layer to the edge of the second layer.
2. Then cut wedge-shaped pieces as shown.

3. When these pieces have been served, do the same with the middle layer. Cut vertically around at the edge of the top layer.
4. Then cut wedge-shaped pieces as shown.

5. When those pieces have been served, return to the bottom layer.
6. Repeat the cuts made in steps 2 and 4.
7. The remaining tiers may be cut into desired-size pieces. Bon appetit!

Preserving the Top Layer

Traditionally, the bride and groom preserve the top tier of their wedding cake so that they can eat it on their first anniversary. If this is your intention, refrigeration alone isn't going to cut it. Taking the following measures should ensure that you'll have an edible cake come your first anniversary.

1. Wrap it tightly in plastic.
2. Place it in a sturdy box.
3. Wrap it in plastic again.
4. Store in freezer.

When the time to eat your cake is upon you, thaw it in the wrappings for approximately 12 hours, then simply unwrap and enjoy!

CHAPTER SEVENTEEN

Party Attire

Bride's Attire

Shopping for your fairy-tale wedding gown can be a long and taxing process. On top of the imposing proposition of finding the ideal gown, there is the added headache of dealing with bridal shop policies, politics, and potential disasters. Have you ever met a bride whose dress was not ready in time for her wedding? How about one who had the flimsy material of her gown rip as she was stepping out of the limousine? Even if you haven't, you can probably say with confidence that these "mishaps" are no one's idea of a good time.

How can you protect yourself? First, shop at only reputable places. If friends and family can't recommend a shop to you, check the pages of your local phone directory and visit area wedding expos. Once you find a place you're seriously considering doing business with, ask for references from former customers and check with the Better Business Bureau to verify that no complaints have been filed against the company.

You should begin shopping as soon as you become engaged. Ideally, you'll order your gown six to nine months before the wedding, as some gowns can take that long to arrive back from the manufacturer. With additional time required for alterations, you could still be cutting it a little close. If you don't have the luxury of that much time, there are shops that can turn around an order in three months, but they may have you pay for the express service, and you may not be able to order your first choice gown. If you decide to buy a discontinued or used gown, time is less of a problem; you just need to concern yourself with getting the alterations completed.

Other gown shopping tips to be aware (and beware) of:

- Always talk to the manager of the shop. Find out how long the place has been in business. (You would hope that a disreputable establishment would not be around long.)
- Be careful of counterfeit gowns. Some shops will tell you they carry brand-name merchandise, when in fact the gowns are cheap imitations, sold to you at an "uncheap" price. (Call the dress manufacturer to verify that the shop is one of their authorized dealers.)
- Choose a delivery date for your gown that is several weeks before the wedding. (This should give you plenty of breathing room for alterations.)
- Make sure that the bridal shop doesn't try to get you to order a size that is much too big for you (i.e., a size 12 gown when you normally take a 4—that way you pay a small fortune for alterations.
- Don't allow the shop to use cloth measuring tapes. Over time, the cloth begins to stretch, often yielding incorrect measurements.
- Ask for verification of your order; call periodically to check on progress. (Sometimes the shops will hold your cash deposit for months before actually ordering your gown.)
- Get a written contract containing every aspect of your purchase agreement, including delivery date, cost of dress, cost of alterations, and any stipulations for refunds if the dress is not ready in time.

If you decide to forgo the bridal shop route and have your dress made by a private seamstress, you should still guard yourself against the typical pitfalls. In addition, you may have to order your dress as much as a year in advance of your wedding, as that is how long it can take to make a gown from scratch.

Bridal Bargains

If you're in the market for an inexpensive dress, your bridal shop's discontinued rack is not necessarily your sole option. The following alternatives to high-end retail have all been known to pay off in major wedding day savings. Just remember, always check for quality: there should be no stains, rips, or other major flaws.

Heirloom/Antique Gowns

With the price of most antiques these days, you wouldn't think an antique (or heirloom) gown would be a bargain, but it can be. Antique and heirloom gowns can be significantly less expensive than new ones, and the added style and nostalgia they provide is beyond price. Unless you're fairly petite, though, you may have a hard time finding one that will fit. Apparently, women were a lot smaller all those years ago.

Used/Consignment Gowns

Another way to get an inexpensive gown (provided you don't care if you're not the first and only person to wear it) is to shop the consignment stores and other bargain outlets for previously worn gowns. These dresses can be bought for as little as $100 and can be taken home with you that day. Of course, finding a quality wedding gown on consignment may require some tenacity and detective work on your part, since these don't come down the pike everyday. If you're serious about taking the previously worn route, check the classified section of the local paper. You might even ask a newly married acquaintance if she feels like selling you her gown (at a huge discount, of course).

Outlet/Warehouse Sales

Perhaps you've seen TV news coverage of a local warehouse's one-day wedding gown sale? Brides-to-be line up as early as six o'clock in the morning to get first crack at wedding gowns, many boasting top designer names, marked down as low as $100 each. It sounds great, but watch out, bargain hunting can be a full contact sport. When the doors open at nine, it's as if a dam had burst. A flood of women cascades through the store to maul the inventory. In this maelstrom, women grab as many dresses as they can carry, irrespective of size, to increase the odds of finding a keeper. No one bothers much with dressing rooms, either, so if you're the modest type, be forewarned: women try dresses on right next to the rack. If the stress and the every-woman-for-herself atmosphere doesn't scare you off, you may very well walk away with a brand new, top-quality gown. Just make sure to show up bright and early (at least an hour before doors open) to get your fair shot at the pick of the litter.

Rent-a-Gown

Another increasingly popular way to find a gown is to rent one. Again, this option is not for someone who cares about being the first to wear the gown, or who wants to keep it to treasure forever. Like a tuxedo rental, the gown is yours only for the wedding, then it's back on the rack for someone else. Through rental, the average gown can

be had for as little as $100; a famous-maker extravaganza that would cost thousands to purchase can be rented for only a few hundred.

The major kink in the rental game: if the gown you choose requires major alteration, they may not let you rent it. Think of how much valuable material would be lost in trying to fit a size 12 to a size 4 woman. After that, the dress could only be rented to very small women, a prospect the shop is unlikely to welcome.

They're Not Just for Bridesmaids Anymore

If you're feeling creative (and a little more handy with a needle and thread than the average bride-to-be), an inexpensive alternative to a formal bridal gown is to get an elegant bridesmaid's dress in white. All you'll have to do is dress it up a bit with some lace, buttons, and the like. It probably won't satisfy you for a formal wedding, but for a more informal event it can be a thrifty and inventive way to go.

The Perfect Gown

What type of gown will you be looking for at the bridal shop or the seamstresses? Most likely long and white, but after that basic decision is taken care of, the choices will appear virtually endless. As a guideline, you might want to consider the degree of formality of your wedding, and, of course, your own personal taste.

Informal wedding:
- Formal, lacy suit or formal street-length gown
- Corsage or small bouquet
- No veil or train

Semiformal wedding:
- Chapel veil and modest bouquet
  (with floor-length gown)
- Shorter fingertip veil or wide-brimmed hat and small
  bouquet (with tea-length or mid-calf-length gown)

Formal daytime wedding:
- Traditional floor-length gown
- Fingertip veil or hat
- Chapel or sweep train
- Gloves
- Medium-size bouquet

Formal evening wedding:
(Same as formal daytime except:)
- Longer veil

Very formal wedding:
- Traditional floor-length gown (usually pure white
  or off-white) with cathedral train or extended
  cathedral train
- Long sleeves or long arm-covering gloves
- Full-length veil
- Elaborate headpiece
- Cascade bouquet

The Crowning Touch: Headpieces and Veils

Your headpiece and/or veil should complement your gown. There are plenty of options out there to choose from, but don't be shocked at the high price tags, which border on the outrageous.

Although a headpiece/veil typically takes only eight to ten weeks to arrive after being ordered, you should consider placing your order even earlier. Having your headpiece or veil early will give you the luxury of a few trial runs with your hairdresser, to ensure you'll get the look you want.

Shop:_____

Contact person:_____

Headpiece description:_____

_____

Cost: _____

Wedding Party Attire

The bride has the privilege of selecting the final choice of fabric, color, and style for the attendants' dresses. Generally, the bridesmaids are dressed alike, but there is also the option of having the dresses differ in style, color, or both! Going this route makes it a lot easier to make every one happy, as a dress that looks great on one woman can look like a potato sack on another. You can also have only the maid/matron of honor wear a different gown, to make her stand out more from the other attendants.

Try to keep in mind the following suggestions when shopping with your attendants.

- 🐾 Check the formal dress section of a quality department store in your area before you go to a bridal salon. You may find appropriate dresses there that your attendants can wear again in the future—and at a cheaper price than salon dresses.
- 🐾 The attendants' dresses should complement your gown.
- 🐾 Ask the attendants' opinions before deciding on a dress. Make sure the gown is one that looks good on everybody. (They are paying for this thing.)
- 🐾 Try to keep the cost of the gown within reason.
- 🐾 If all of your attendants' shoes have to be dyed the same color, it is best to have them dyed together, to ensure an exact color match.

The Flower Girl

You may want the flower girl's dress to match the attendants' dresses—or to be completely different. The dress may be short or floor length, according to the style you want. If you have trouble finding something, a fancy party dress is a good—and inexpensive—choice.

The Groom and His Attendants

Formal Wear

These days, the groom and his attendants usually rent their formal wear. There are formal wear choices available to match the style demands of most weddings. All the men need to do is tell the store attendant what they're in the market for and they're in business.

Informal wedding:

- 🐾 Business suit
- 🐾 White dress shirt and tie
- 🐾 Black shoes and dark socks (For the winter, consider dark colors; in the summer, navy, white, and lighter colors are appropriate.)

Semiformal wedding (daytime):

- 🐾 Dark formal suit jacket (in summer, select a lighter shade)
- 🐾 Dark trousers
- 🐾 White dress shirt
- 🐾 Cummberbund or vest
- 🐾 Four-in-hand or bow tie
- 🐾 Black shoes and dark socks

Semiformal wedding (evening):

- 🐾 Formal suit or dinner jacket with matching trousers (preferably black)
- 🐾 Cummerbund or vest
- 🐾 Black bow tie
- 🐾 White shirt
- 🐾 Cufflinks and studs

Formal wedding (daytime):

- 🐾 Cutaway or stroller jacket in gray or black
- 🐾 Waistcoat (usually grey)
- 🐾 Striped trousers
- 🐾 White high-collared (wing-collared) shirt
- 🐾 Striped tie
- 🐾 Studs and cufflinks

Formal wedding (evening):

- 🐾 Black dinner jacket and trousers
- 🐾 Black bow tie

- White tuxedo shirt
- Waistcoat
- Cummerbund or vest
- Cufflinks

Very formal wedding (daytime):

- Cutaway coat (black or gray)
- Wing-collared shirt
- Ascot
- Striped trousers
- Cufflinks
- Gloves

Very formal wedding (evening):

- Black tailcoat
- Matching striped trousers trimmed with satin
- White bow tie
- White wing-collared shirt
- White waistcoat
- Patent leather shoes
- Studs and cufflinks
- Gloves

Ringbearer/Trainbearer

Most often the ringbearer and trainbearer are little boys, but they probably enjoy being dressed like the big guys. In most weddings, the ringbearer and trainbearers wear the same basic outfit as the rest of the men (only in a much smaller size) or a slight variation of the outfit featuring knickers or shorts.

The men should rent their formal wear one to three months before the wedding. Although a month is usually enough time to reserve the clothing in the "off season," it's better to be early and safe during peak wedding months (April–October). Obviously, the men should do business at a reputable shop, not one that will forget their order and rent out all of their tuxedos to prom-going high schoolers the morning of your wedding.

CHAPTER EIGHTEEN

Queen for a Day: Wedding Day Beauty Tips

ave you ever been warned never to get your hair cut before getting your picture taken because "you'll look like a stranger in your own hair"? It's true; we all feel somewhat self-conscious after going under the scissors for a drastic cut. Needless to add, none of us wants that feeling translated forever onto film. This advice goes double, nay quintuple, for your wedding. Never get a haircut or change your hair-style right before your wedding. Not only do you run the risk of "looking like a stranger in your own hair," but you might wind up hating your new coif and feeling miserable on your big day.

Believe it or not, getting a facial on the day of your wedding, or anytime close to it, is also ill-advised. Most professional facials are not given with a light touch. They involve rigorous cleansing methods that can leave skin looking blotchy, reddened, or even damaged. If you do want a facial, be sure to schedule it at least a week or two in advance. The same goes for tanning beds, which should not be used either the day of or the day before the wedding. Waxing facial hair should also be done in advance due to the temporary irritation and blotchiness that this harsh treatment may inflict upon your otherwise radiant visage.

Facials, waxes, artificial tans, and drastic haircuts aside, there is no proper or improper way to go about pampering yourself on your wedding day. If you feel confident in your ability to style your own hair, apply your own cosmetics, and do your own nails, there's no need to make a trip to the salon on your wedding day. Of course, if you're anything at all like the majority of brides, you'll reach for the security of professional stylists come wedding day.

Hair, Beautiful Hair!

Brides walking out of a salon, hair all done up, headpiece in place, wearing jeans and a T-shirt (which will have to be cut off later to keep from ruining the hair do) are a humorous but not uncommon sight. If you don't want to be seen in public this way, see whether your hairdresser would be willing to make the trip to your home, or wherever you may be getting ready that day.

Hair Do's

- Make an appointment to consult with your hairdresser
- Bring your headpiece and ask the stylist to work around it. Try a few different styles on for size.
- If you like the do and don't feel comfortable doing it yourself, make an appointment to get your hair done on your wedding day.
- Ask the hairdresser if you have to make the trek to the salon or if he/she would be able to come to you. How much extra would this cost? Do you have to pay more for work that runs overtime, and how much?
- Make sure the hairdresser knows exactly where and when to meet you.
- Wear a button-down shirt when getting your hair styled. There's nothing worse than suddenly realizing you're going to have to cut yourself out of your favorite shirt, or ruin your hair pulling your shirt over your head.

Put on a Happy Face

Like your hairdresser, a cosmetologist can help you feel more confident in your appearance, or give you a completely new look. Even if you're already satisfied with your daily makeup selection and application skills, you may want to try something different, something special for your wedding day. Think of your face as a blank canvas and your cosmetologist as a renowned artist. He or she can show you just what colors to apply, what angles to apply them at, and other tricks to make your face into a real masterpiece.

To get a new look for your wedding, you can either enlist the services of a professional cosmetologist or a department store cosmetologist. While you can get lucky with the latter, your safest bet is the professional variety who are employed by reputable beauty salons. Sure, a professional will cost you a little more, but at least they won't make you look like a circus clown while trying to sell you a lot of products that you may not need.

Makeup Do's

- Schedule a consultation with a trusted makeup artist in your price range.
- Go in for a practice session, just so there are no surprises come wedding day.
- If you like the makeup job performed by the cosmetologist, make an appointment for the day of your wedding.
- Ask if the cosmetologist can do your makeup at your home? If yes, how much would this service cost?

Nail Polish

Even if you've always considered manicures to be frivolous, you might want to make an exception for your wedding day. Just consider this: after admiring your dress, your hair, and your new husband, friends and family are going to want to see your ring finger. Or, your photographer might

suggest a "ring shot," where you and your groom clasp left hands over your bouquet. How are you going to feel with all those eyes staring at your fingers?

If your regular toilet routine includes caring for your nails, then you shouldn't need any special attention. Just make an appointment with your emory board—or get your handy-with-a-nail-file mom or maid of honor to help out—and you're good to go. However, if you're worried that your fingernails will look misshapen, bitten, or just plain unattractive, you might want to splurge on a manicure the day before or the day of the wedding. Here are your options:

A French manicure
Accents the white half moons at the tips of your finger nails and gives them a high buff. This option costs a little more but is well worth the time and expense.

Acrylics
Real-looking faux nails. If you're a biter, this is the way to go.

Standard
Shapes and polishes the nails.

Colors
Stick with subtle shades such as sheer pink or off white. Stay away from the fire-engine reds and the off-beat brights; these colors might be fun for the honey-moon, but they would probably raise eyebrows during the ceremony.

Wedding Emergency Kit

Make up a wedding day emergency kit and put someone reliable in charge of bringing it wherever you go. What goes in such a wedding first-aid kit? Here are some must-haves:

- [ ] Extra makeup
- [ ] Nylons
- [ ] Needles
- [ ] Thread
- [ ] Bridal-shop recommended stain treatment
- [ ] Aspirin (and other necessary medications)
- [ ] Hairspray
- [ ] Brush or comb
- [ ] Breath mints (just in case)

CHAPTER NINETEEN

Bon Voyage! A Hassle-Free Honeymoon

hat with all the frenzied planning, coordinating, organizing, and worrying involved, getting yourself married can be a full-time job—and then some! When it's all over with, you'll need more than just an ordinary vacation to recuperate.

On the surface, a honeymoon is no different from any other vacation you might take. You pack your bags, make your reservations, and leave home for fun in the sun, snow, or whatever. But lets face it, to a pair of newlyweds, a honeymoon is much more than that; it's their first getaway together as a married couple, and perhaps the ultimate romantic experience. Ten years from now, you probably won't recall just when it was you spent that summer week in the mountains or that long weekend skiing. But you're bound to remember nearly every detail about your honeymoon, wherever you may go.

Decisions, Decisions!

If you and your fiancé are having trouble settling on a destination, it might be a good idea to consider the most popular honeymoon spots. After all, the reservation agents won't wait forever; some of the most vied-after destinations may be booked up to a year in advance. Use the following lists to help you in your decision-making process and pick a place in no time.

In the Caribbean:
- Aruba
- Cayman Islands
- Little Dix Bay, British Virgin Islands
- Montego Bay, Jamaica
- Nassau, Bahamas
- Negril, Jamaica
- Ocho Rios, Jamaica
- Paradise Island, Bahamas
- St. Croix

In Mexico:
- Baja California region
- Cancun, Quintana Roo
- Guadalajara, Jalisco
- Isla de Cozumel, Quintana Roo
- Puerta Vallarta, Jalisco

In the South Pacific:
- The Marquesas
- Tahiti

In Europe:
- Greece
- Spain
- England
- France
- Italy
- Germany
- Austria
- Switzerland
- Sweden
- Finland
- Norway
- Monaco

In the United States:
- Alaska
- Hawaii
- Grand Canyon National Park, Arizona
- Niagara Falls, New York
- The California Pacific Coast Highway
- Hilton Head, South Carolina
- Poconos Mountains, Pennsylvania
- Disneyland, Anaheim, California
- Walt Disney World, Orlando, Florida
- Massachusetts Beach Resorts: Cape Cod, Martha's Vineyard, and Nantucket
- U.S. Virgin Islands

Note: Don't forget about more exotic locations like:
- Australia
- the Netherlands
- Japan
- South America
- Africa
- India

Saver's Fares

While perusing through your honeymoon options, you might find that your budget has as much of an impact on your final destination as your dreams. Of course, this is hardly a reason to call the whole thing off. Provided you do a little research, you can have your honeymoon and your money too.

Here are a list of places to consult for inexpensive travel arrangements.

- Travel agents
- Internet travel sites
- Travel books
- Travel magazines
- Travel section in newspaper

Look for the following:
- Low-priced airfares
- Reduced-rate hotel/airfare package deals
- Alternative accommodations
  - apartment swaps
  - hostels
  - bed and breakfasts

Plan Ahead

Perhaps you're used to handling your vacation arrangements by yourself, without the help of a travel agent. If you're going out of the country, however, you may wish to work with an agent to help you figure out the nuances of international travel. Because foreign vacations can get very complicated—with connecting flights that have to meet boats that have to meet trains (you get the picture)—letting all the responsibility fall squarely in the lap of a trained agent may be a good idea. After all, don't you have more than enough to do just with planning the wedding?

Your agent will tell you what paperwork, identification, and other necessities you will need in order to travel abroad. With the exception of Canada, Mexico, and some parts of the Caribbean, you'll need a passport, which takes at least six weeks (and sometimes longer) to obtain. Here are some other documents you will need that may take some time to track down.

- 🐾 Birth certificate
- 🐾 Driver's license (or other picture ID)
- 🐾 Proof of marriage
- 🐾 Proof of citizenship

Pack Your Bags!

Ideally, you should pack for your trip a few days before the wedding (a week beforehand is probably best, but let's face it, that's unrealistic). Don't get caught running around the house in your wedding gown, throwing clothes into suitcases while you wait for your limo to arrive. Never mind the stress, think of the potential consequences: It's hard to get cozy with your new hubby if you've forgotten to pack the toothbrushes or deodorant.

Haste can make for forgetfulness, so plan well and plan early. Once you're at your honeymoon destination, your poor, planned-out body and mind won't have to plan anything else. Toward that end, here's a list of forget-me-nots:

For your carry-on bag:
- [ ] Tickets
- [ ] Traveler's checks
- [ ] Driver's licenses
- [ ] Proof of age and citizenship
- [ ] Passports, visas (if appropriate)
- [ ] List of luggage contents (for insurance purposes if luggage is lost or stolen)
- [ ] Name and phone number of someone to contact in case of emergency
- [ ] Checking account numbers (kept separate from checks)
- [ ] Eyewear
- [ ] Any medication
- [ ] Valuable jewelry
- [ ] Marriage license
- [ ] Birth control
- [ ] List of credit card numbers

For your suitcase:
- [ ] Camera
- [ ] Film (and plenty of it)
- [ ] Batteries (for camera)
- [ ] Cosmetics
- [ ] Deodorant
- [ ] Hair dryer
- [ ] Corkscrew or bottle opener
- [ ] Shampoo
- [ ] Conditioner
- [ ] Toothbrushes and toothpaste
- [ ] Disposable razors (and blades)
- [ ] Q-tips
- [ ] Nail clippers or scissors
- [ ] First-aid kit
- [ ] Feminine hygiene products
- [ ] Pain reliever
- [ ] Antacids
- [ ] Vitamins

For the beach:
- [ ] Bathing suits
- [ ] Sandals
- [ ] Coverups
- [ ] Sunscreen and tanning lotion
- [ ] Sunglasses
- [ ] Beach bag

For the snow:
- [ ] Winter jacket
- [ ] Hats
- [ ] Boots
- [ ] Gloves
- [ ] Sweaters
- [ ] Thick socks
- [ ] Skis (if you have them)

The Fine Art of Tipping

When, whom, and how much to tip are often embarrassing and confusing questions. In some situations you can ask your companions at the dining table in a hotel or on shipboard, or the management, but it's better to be prepared with some knowledge of the travel tipping structure.

Tipping on a Cruise Line

- Room steward: cleans your cabin, makes the bed, supplies towels, soap, ice, and room service. Tip: $3.50 per day per person. Tip at the end of the trip. Some also tip on the first day, "to ensure the perfect service"—a slogan said to be the origin of the word *tips*.

- Dining room waiter and busboy: waiter, $3.50 per person per day, half that for the busboy.

- Bartenders, wine steward, pool and deck attendants, etc.: check the bar bill. On almost all ships, a service charge is automatically added, making a tip unnecessary. Other service personnel should be tipped when the service is given, at the same rate as for service ashore, usually 15 percent.

- Maitre d', headwaiter: in charge of the dining room. No tip is necessary unless he has handled special requests for you.

- "No-tipping" ships: some cruise lines advertise a "no-tip" policy. People still tip for special services on such ships, but it is not necessary if you do not ask for anything "above and beyond."

Tipping at the Airport

- The porter: $1 per bag when you check in at the curb or have bags taken to check in for you. Obviously, if you go the DIY route, no tip is necessary or expected.

Tipping at the Hotel

- Bellboy: $1 per bag, plus $1 for hospitable gestures—turning on lights, opening windows. Tip on service.

- Chambermaid: $1 for each service, minimum $5 per couple per week. Tip each day; a new chambermaid may be assigned during your stay.

- Doorman: $1 per bag; $1 for hailing a taxi. Tip on service.

- Headwaiter: $5 per week for special service, $2–$3 for regular service—tip on your first day.

- Wait staff: 15 to 20 percent of the bill when no service charge is added; some add 5 percent when there is a service charge. Tip at each meal.

- Room Service: 15 to 20 percent of bill in addition to room service charge. If the menu or bill explicitly states that a gratuity will automatically be added, you might add an additional $1 or refrain from tipping altogether.

- Other service personnel: the general rule to follow is to tip 15 percent to 20 percent of the bill, unless the person serving you owns the business. Some owner-hairdressers, for example, do not accept tips, but charge more for their services.

CHAPTER TWENTY

"The Name Game"

*W*hat's in a name? For years you may have taken your own surname for granted. But faced with its possible loss, you may find yourself more attached to the old name than you'd realized. This is the name you went through school with, the name you went to work with, the name you made friends with, the name everyone knows you by. It feels like a part of you. How can you let it go?

On the other hand, maybe your last name is 10 syllables long. Or, you've yet to meet anyone who's ever been able to pronounce or spell it right. So, you're only to happy to take the name of your husband-to-be. If this is an easy decision, congratulations! Your task is much simpler than a lot of people's. For many brides, however, the decision is quite difficult. If you are in a quandary over this issue, remember that these days the only people who will probably care about it are you, your husband, and your immediate families. In other words, there's no reason to spend lots of energy worrying "What will people think?"

Your Good Name and How to Keep It

The following list covers all the options available to those women who like their last name and have no intention of parting with it.

- Use your maiden name as your middle name and your husband's as your last. So, if Jennifer Andrews married Richard Miller, she'd be Jennifer Andrews Miller.
- Hyphenate the two last names: Jennifer Andrews-Miller. This means that the two separate last names are now joined to make one name (kind of like a marriage). You keep your regular middle

name, but saying your full name can be a mouthful. Jennifer Marie Andrews-Miller.

- ℘ Take your husband's name legally, but use your maiden name professionally. In everyday life and social situations, you'd use your married name, but in the office, you'd use the same name you always had.

- ℘ Hyphenate both your and your husband's last names: Jennifer Andrews-Miller and Richard Andrews-Miller

- ℘ Agree to drop both your names and create an entirely new last name out of the two, such as Milland.

- ℘ Have your husband-to-be take your surname.

The Change of a Lifetime

If one or both of you will be changing your name after marriage, you should be sure to update the following:

☐ 401(k) accounts	☐ Loans
☐ Automotive insurance	☐ Medical insurance
☐ Bank accounts	☐ Other insurance accounts
☐ Billing accounts	☐ Passport
☐ Car registration	☐ Pension plan records
☐ Club membership	☐ Post office
☐ Credit cards	☐ Property titles
☐ Dentist	☐ Safety deposit box
☐ Doctors	☐ School records
☐ Driver's license	☐ Social security
☐ Employment records	☐ Stocks and bonds
☐ Homeowner's/ renter's insurance	☐ Subscriptions
☐ IRA accounts	☐ Telephone listing
☐ Leases	☐ Voter registration records
☐ Life insurance	☐ Wills/trusts
	☐ Other (list below)

No Loose Ends:
Last Minute Preparations

Although you've probably taken care of all the details by this late date, there's something to be said for the kind of peace of mind that only comes by double-checking. Many of the following tasks may be (and probably should be) attended to in the days just before your wedding. Of course, if you try to accomplish them all up to a week before the wedding, you'll have that much more opportunity to relax and enjoy your last week of single life.

❑ Make sure the following people all know the correct locations and times. Reconfirm plans with your:
  - officiant
  - reception site coordinator
  - photographer
  - videographer
  - band/DJ
  - florist
  - baker
  - limousine company
  - hair stylist
❑ Reconfirm your honeymoon travel arrangements and hotel reservations.
❑ Reconfirm your hotel reservation for your wedding night.
❑ Make sure your wedding attendants know where they need to be and when, and remind them of any special duties they need to perform (see pages 12–15).
❑ Finish any last-minute packing

- ❏ Pack your going-away outfit and accessories. If you'll be changing at the reception site, put a trusted friend in charge of making sure they arrive there safely.
- ❏ Give your wedding rings and marriage license to your honor attendants to hold until the ceremony.
- ❏ Make sure your groom and best man have enough cash for tipping.
- ❏ Give an "emergency repair kit" (safety pins, extra hosiery, tissues, aspirin, etc.) to a trusted attendant, so you'll be better prepared to deal with the unexpected.
- ❏ Make sure your honeymoon luggage is stored in the trunk of your "getaway car" or is sent ahead to wherever you're spending your wedding night.
- ❏ Arrange for a friend to drive your car to the reception site if you intend to drive yourselves to the hotel or inn where you'll be staying.

Index